GUNS DON'T DIE—PEOPLE DO

GUNS DON'T

DIE—

PEOPLE DO

PETE SHIELDS

Chairman, Handgun Control, Inc.
with John Greenya

ARBOR HOUSE New York

DEDICATED TO

the memory of our Nick

and to the thousands and thousands of other young Americans
lost to our nation's tragic level of handgun violence.

And to my wife Jeanne and our other children, Pam, David,
and Leslie, for accepting with such grace the many changes in
our lives this fight has required of us.

Grateful acknowledgment is made to Ann Landers and Field
Newspaper Syndicate for permission to reprint the column on
page 152, copyright © Field Newspaper Syndicate.

ACKNOWLEDGMENTS

THIS book could not have become a reality without the talented and patient collaboration of John Greenya, the dedicated help of Charles Orasin, Handgun Control, Inc.'s tireless Vice President, and the skilled manuscript preparation of Barbara Lautman and Amy Apperson.

Handgun Control, Inc. itself could never have developed into the force it is without the vision, persistence, and help of many, many dedicated friends and associates.

First among all must be Mark Borinsky, whose vision, initiative, and determination made all that followed possible; and then Ed Welles, the organization's first Executive Director, and continual counselor, friend, and director in the largest sense of those words. And, as with this book, Handgun Control, Inc. would not be what it is today without the skills and dedicated services of Charles Orasin.

The list of those whose encouragement, persistence, time, talent, and labors (rewarded or unrewarded) helped make Handgun Control, Inc. happen is endless. But I must mention:

The many members of our Board.

The law firms that helped us, either to get started or to stay alive and grow: Covington & Burling; Wilmer, Cutler & Pickering (especially Jim Campbell and his team); and Fried, Frank, Harris, Shriver & Kampleman.

Roger Craver and Tom Mathews for showing us the way, and for their personal friendship.

My good friends and political counselors John Craig and Doug Bailey.

The audio-visual help of my many friends at Lyon's Studios in Wilmington, with special thanks to Mike Keel.

The many staff members of Handgun Control, Inc., who are giving or have given us so much commitment over the years.

The tireless commitment of *all* our volunteers but especially Henry Bashkin, Kay Erstein, and Harriet Rugh who have been with us almost from the beginning.

No Handgun Control, Inc. acknowledgments would be complete or sufficient without our sincere and heartfelt thanks to the many hundreds of victims of handgun violence who have been willing to join us in going public with their tragedies, by making their tragedies America's tragedies and thus helping to create a less violent America for the future.

My sincere thanks to you all, including our many generous financial supporters, Handgun Control, Inc. members, and friends. Our hope for a saner, safer America exists because of you.

CONTENTS

poster tells it all: "Stop Handguns Before They Stop You."

Charles Ticho, Lois Hess, Peggy Anderson. A boost
from Ann Landers.

The high cost of fear in America. Key provisions of
the Kennedy-Rodino Crime Control Act, which
would stop Saturday Night Specials, require a
waiting period for a check of handgun purchasers,
put criminals behind bars, improve the handgun
record-keeping system, encourage states to pass
license-to-carry laws, and transfer enforcement
responsibility from the Treasury to the Justice
Department.

Michael Halberstam is killed—by handguns.
President Reagan is wounded, but reaffirms his
position. We help defeat one pro-gun control
congressman in the 1980 elections—and strongly
influence others. The new Congress treats us with
more respect. Now, with our numbers increasing,
they know we *will not* go away.

INTRODUCTION

O N April 16, 1974, at approximately 9:30 p.m. in San Francisco, California, my twenty-three-year-old son Nick was shot to death. At the time it happened, his mother and I were at our home in Wilmington, Delaware, where we had raised all four of our children. We were asleep.

Like so many bright young people in the late '60's and early '70's, Nick Shields had dropped out of college after a couple of years to "find himself." For six months he'd worked in Colorado as a carpenter's helper and then as a short-order cook at a ski resort (so he could afford to ski every day). Then he'd decided to come back east and get a degree in photography.

While waiting to see if he had been accepted at the Rochester Institute of Technology, Nick decided to drive to California and see his sister and some friends before heading home. Leaving his skis with friends, he piled the rest of his few belongings in his beat-up old car and headed for California, accompanied by Lady, a nondescript black dog he'd adopted. Because his sister Pam lived near Los Angeles, Nick made his first stop the San Francisco area where he had a pair of special friends, Ginna and Sheldon Crosby.

Virginia ("Ginna") Weir had grown up with Nick in Wilmington, and they had remained close friends. When she married Sheldon Crosby, Nick and Sheldon also became friends.

Nick liked the little houseboat community in Sausalito where the Crosbys lived. And he liked their friends. There was the

11

friendly Chinese neighbor on one side, and there was also Jonathan May, a graduate student with whom Sheldon relaxed by playing lacrosse, which happened to be Nick's favorite sport—after skiing. When they learned that Nick had been captain of his high-school lacrosse team, they asked Nick if he'd like to work out with their team, the Golden Gate Lacrosse Club.

Those enticements, plus the fact that the Crosbys' houseboat was literally about to sink and they needed a carpenter's help, convinced Nick he should stay in San Francisco a bit longer.

On Tuesday, April 16, in the late afternoon, Nick and Jon May left Sausalito in the Crosbys' Vega station wagon, and drove across the Golden Gate Bridge for a lacrosse practice in Funston Park. After it was over, they headed for the home of a friend of Jon's to pick up a rug he had bought.

When they got there, Nick began to straighten out the back of the wagon, which was cluttered with sports gear, while Jon went in the house to get the rug.

I don't know whether or not Nick was aware of the so-called "Zebra killings," a wave of senseless, brutal attacks and murders that had plagued the city since the previous October. (The police said the name "Zebra" came from the radio channel used exclusively for communications relating to the series of random attacks, but others suggested it stemmed from the fact that all the victims were white, and all the killers reportedly black.) But the street where they stopped was not in a rough area, and I doubt any thoughts of the Zebra killers even crossed Nick's mind.

As he stood there rearranging the lacrosse gear, a man walked up behind him, took a handgun from inside his jacket, and shot Nick three times in the back. My son pitched forward against the car, fell back, and then slumped to the street where he died instantly, lacrosse stick in hand.

The phone call from California came after one in the morning, Delaware time. But it did not come, as one might expect from seeing movies and television shows, from anyone in a position of authority. Instead, it came from our Wilmington neighbor, Bob Weir, whose daughter Ginna had called him from Sausalito and asked him to be the one to break the news to us. In addition to being our friend, Bob Weir was Nick's godfather.

As soon as I was conscious of the fact that my sleep was being interrupted by a ringing phone, I took a fast mental inventory—

as one does almost instinctively when the phone rings in the middle of the night—of the children's whereabouts. Pam was in California; Nick was in Colorado—no, wait, he was in California too; David was at Rutgers; and Leslie was also in school outside Boston. I pulled myself to a sitting position and reached for the phone.

"Pete? This is Bob. Are you awake?"

I mumbled something to the effect that I was getting there, and then Bob said:

"Are you sitting down?"

With that, I of course knew something was wrong. But my imagination never conceived that it could be anything like what it was.

Bob then began to talk, and he talked nonstop, very fast, a blue streak, telling me everything he knew about what had happened. He didn't give me a chance to interrupt him, and I think now it was because he was afraid that if he stopped he wouldn't be able to continue. So he told me the whole story, as he knew it, from beginning to end without interruption.

Finally, because I could literally *feel* Jeanne's eyes on my back, I cut in for the first time and said the only words I said throughout that phone call: "Bob, I have to call you back, I have to stop now. Jeanne's awake and I have to tell her."

Bob replied, "Don't worry about calling back. We're not going to go back to bed now. And if you want us to come over we will."

I put down the phone and turned to Jeanne, who by this time was sitting up in bed too. I do not recall exactly what I said, but I believe it was just "Nick's dead." She screamed. And then I told her everything Bob Weir had told me.

How we got through the next hour, and exactly what we said and did, I do not know. (What would you do if someone told you one of your children had been killed?) I do know that shortly before two o'clock, one of us realized that because of the three-hour time difference, unless we reached our daughter Pam right away, she would probably learn of her brother's death by hearing it on the eleven o'clock news. Although it took some doing, we were able to track her down—she was with friends, thank God—before the news of Nick's killing came on the air.

By that point we had gotten up, dressed, and faced the fact—as well as it can ever be faced, either in a brief period of time or in months and years—that our son was dead.

Sometime between two and three in the morning the Weirs

arrived. Not only had the four of us been friends for years, but so had our children, as we had taken vacations together. And of all the children the closest had been Nick and Ginna.

So what we talked about, through the small hours of that terrible night, was Nick and Ginna, and all the good times they'd had. Eventually we even got photographs out, and there was even laughter now and then as we viewed a particularly funny and familiar snapshot.

We still had not yet heard from any San Francisco official. Although I had no illusions, I thought it would be best if I talked to someone in an official capacity out there who could verify Nick's death and tell me *exactly* what had happened.

So I called the chief of police's office, to be told by a not very sympathetic aide that it was the coroner's job to verify death. He did, however, say that he would contact the coroner and have him call me, which he did. When the coroner called he explained, rather lamely, I thought, that he hadn't called me personally because "the girl who knew him said she would do it." He meant Ginna Crosby.

Soon after the Weirs arrived, the first of the phone calls from the media began to come in, the Zebra killings being a national news story, and they were not easy to deal with. Around seven, a number of friends arrived. One of them worked in public relations for Du Pont. He announced that he would handle all calls from the media, which was a godsend as he knew exactly what to say.

Sometime before seven a.m., we realized with a start that if we didn't inform Nick's grandfathers right away they would probably hear it on the morning news. We called Jeanne's father and mine. My father had been particularly fond of Nick, and not simply because he bore the same name, and I was worried about the effect of the news on him. As it turned out, I was right to be worried; Nick's death, and the circumstances of it, seemed to destroy his interest in life. He died several months later.

Shortly after seven, just as soon as it was practical to do so, we called David's and Leslie's schools and began the process of getting them home just as soon as possible. Then friends who had heard of Nick's death on the morning news started arriving.

At this point decisions had to be made, and we had to grapple with problems of time and distance. Nick's body was 3,000 miles from home. Would he be buried or cremated? If cremated, should that be done in California or back home? If he were cremated in California, should all of us fly out there, because if we didn't it would mean not seeing Nick one last time. And if we decided not to fly the entire family to San Francisco, should both Jeanne and I go? Should it just be me?

In trying to decide what to do about going to California, and all the related questions, we badly missed the counsel of our minister and close personal friend (and next-door neighbor) John O'Hear, who had taken his traditional week-after-Easter vacation. In addition to spiritual and moral support, John could have helped with some of the practical questions. As an ordained Episcopal minister, he had years of experience with times of crisis and the myriad details that have to be dealt with.

Finally, we decided on cremation. Having made that decision, we then decided the best course would be for me to fly to California alone, take care of identifying Nick's body and disposing of his "effects," and then have his body cremated out there. Jeanne would stay in Delaware to be there when David and Leslie arrived home. The tragedy of this decision was that Jeanne would not see Nick again.

At some early point in the morning we received a call from John O'Hear, who'd been notified by someone at the church. John spoke briefly, but his message was tremendously supportive. At the end he said, "When are you going to California?" I told him that we'd just arranged to get me on an 11:00 a.m. flight. He said he had some "thinking" to do and that he'd call me back shortly. Fifteen minutes later, the phone rang and John said, "I'll meet you in San Francisco this afternoon. I've already spoken to the church authorities out there, and they will make all the necessary arrangements."

Suddenly it was time for me to leave. I had almost walked out the door when I realized that I didn't have any money. By this time the house was filled with friends, and they literally passed a hat for me.

Those who'd arranged for my flight had bought me a first-class ticket and also, without telling me, informed the crew why I was making the trip, so I was treated with special care and generally left alone. I was too numb to sleep on the plane, but before I knew it we had landed in Chicago, where the flight took on more passengers for the long leg of the coast-to-coast trip. When a stewardess asked if I wanted anything from the terminal, I said without thinking, "A newspaper." When I opened the paper, the story of Nick's death was on the front page—accompanied by a picture of his dead body lying on the ground.

I threw the paper on the seat beside me and tried to get a grip on myself. My emotions were swirling now, and the question that kept coming back to my mind was so deceptively simple: *Why?* I had no better answer now than I had when Bob Weir called me twelve hours earlier.

Then I realized that if the story of Nick's death had been on the front page of the *Chicago Tribune,* certainly there would be newspeople waiting for me in San Francisco. I had no desire to see the press, yet I had a growing sense that I wanted to say *something,* make some statement about the madness and futility of the act that had taken Nick from all of us.

Nick. Nelson T. Shields, IV. Twenty-three years old. Beloved son of Jeanne Doster Otis Shields and Nelson T. Shields, III. Beloved grandson of Nelson T. Shields, Jr. and of Alexis Doster. Survived by sisters Pamela and Leslie and brother David. Survived by countless friends. Gone. Killed by a stranger whose face he never saw, a stranger who fired three pistol shots into Nick's back.

Airplanes, it seems, are never early, but on that day that airplane was. And because it was early I had a chance to slip past the press, some of whose members I could see running toward the gate where my plane had already arrived. As I walked past a man with press credentials hanging around his neck, I heard him say, "This is one of the most screwed-up assignments I've ever been on. How the hell are we supposed to recognize this Shields?"

The young man with him said, "Well, his son was in his twenties, so he must have gray hair."

As I was still predominantly blond, it was no problem to walk right past them. However, I stopped for a moment to collect my thoughts. Across from me were a group of newspeople setting up lights, TV cameras and tape recorders.

I was caught up in a welter of conflicting emotions: I wanted to avoid the press corps, to say nothing to them, yet at the same time

I suddenly felt that I wanted to scream—to scream through them to the entire country and world. But I had absolutely no idea of the words I would scream. My mind was simply tumbling. To my left was an information booth. All I had to do was walk over there and ask them to page my daughter Pam Shields (who, because my plane was early, had yet to arrive) and the press would find me.

For quite some time I stood there, debating whether or not to walk over to that booth. And then I saw Pam, in the distance, coming down the corridor, and the debate was over.

Pam drove me to the Crosbys' houseboat in Sausalito, where two things in particular touched me. One was the deep feeling and even the unwarranted guilt felt by Jonathan May, the young man who'd been with Nick when he was killed and who felt that if he had somehow done things differently that fateful Tuesday, Nick might still be alive.

The other involved a silent display. As I walked past Nick's old car, still parked in the lot where all the people who lived on the houseboats parked, I saw that it was covered with bouquets of flowers. This was the handiwork of Sylvia, the Chinese girl who lived in a nearby boat, and who was following the Chinese custom of covering the deceased's belongings with garlands of flowers as a sign of respect and love.

That same afternoon John O'Hear arrived. I learned that he had already made all the necessary arrangements regarding the cremation. The next day, after I identified Nick's body, a funeral home would pick him up and deliver him to the crematorium. John had taken care of all the hard, ugly details.

The next morning I identified his body, through a pane of glass, viewing only his head (a sheet kept me from seeing his fatal wounds). Because of the glass, I was not able to touch him.

Once that was over, one of the two police inspectors in charge of the Zebra investigation told me that a mob of media people were waiting down the hall to interview me.

Wavering again in my resolve to say something to them, I asked if there was a way to avoid them.

"Mr. Shields," he replied, "I can keep them out of the building, but I can't keep them off the street outside."

I got his point.

The room used for the press conference was long and narrow. There were no chairs. I entered from the back of the room, accompanied by John O'Hear, who had literally not left my side since he'd arrived in San Francisco. As I started to walk toward the lone table at the far end of the room, I felt him stop. I grabbed for his arm, but he shook his head and told me, "No, this is all yours."

I walked to the front, and stood for a long moment with my hands on the table and my back to the crowd of newspeople. Then I turned and waited for the questions to begin coming. There was a very long silence. It must have been a minute long. Then I realized they were waiting for me to make a statement.

I had no statement prepared, had not even thought of preparing one. I looked to the back and found John O'Hear's eyes locked on mine. He never lost eye contact with me. Even though he was across the room, he was still with me.

I began to talk about Nick, to tell them why he was such a special person, why his death was so terribly senseless. I can't recall what I said exactly, but I know I made the point that Nick was someone who loved people, and that it would be a special tragedy to let the message of his life be snuffed out by a momentary burst of irrational hatred. From time to time I would glance at my friend John O'Hear; he was always with me.

In the middle of my remarks I lost control and became choked up. I could not speak for several moments. To my surprise—and I'm still grateful to them—the reporters turned off their recorders and even their cameras, and waited patiently and silently for me to compose myself. In my opinion that gesture certainly gives the lie to all the stories one hears about the callousness of the media.

When I finished my eulogy to my son, there was a flurry of questions. Several newspeople asked why I, unlike the relatives of other Zebra victims, had said nothing about his killer, why I had not said I wanted to "blow him off the streets." My answer was that I'd not even thought of the killer. All my thoughts had been of Nick.

In addition, they asked three provocative questions. One, was I in favor of capital punishment; two, did Nick use drugs; and, three, did Nick have any strong political involvement (this was the time of Patty Hearst's kidnapping and her alleged espousal of the tenets of the radical SLA)? I answered "no" to all three questions.

Flying home, I thought about the future. As Jeanne would write in *Newsweek* four years later, by which time we were both deeply involved in the fight for handgun control, "No matter how many children you have, the death of one leaves a void that cannot be filled. Life seems to include a new awareness, and one's philosophy and values come under sharper scrutiny. Were we just to pick up the pieces and continue as before? That choice became impossible, because a meaning had to be given to this vicious, senseless death."

I was fifty years old, a marketing manager in the consumer products division at E. I. du Pont de Nemours and Company, and I had the rest of my life to live. But that life, as far as I was concerned, had just changed, had just *been* changed, radically and unalterably. Could I go back to my old way of life? Could Jeanne? Could we live as we had before?

I think that even then, on the way back from the scene of Nick's death, I was beginning to doubt it.

On Saturday, April 20, 1974, the memorial service for Nick was held at our church, Christ Church Christiana Hundred, in Wilmington, Delaware. The church was filled with beautiful flowers from the gardens of our friends.

While he was still in San Francisco, John O'Hear had called the church and arranged that the memorial be a repeat of the Easter Service. That kind of special thoughtfulness was typical of John.

The church was not small, yet it overflowed with people, many of them young friends who had come from distant parts of the country to say good-by to Nick. We had a full communion service, and special prayers were offered by Cal Wick, the assistant minister who worked with the young people of the parish, by his godfather Bob Weir, and by Malcolm Coates, who'd been Nick's headmaster in high school and who had kept in close touch with him. In fact, on the night before he was killed, Nick had had dinner with the Coates' in Palo Alto, where Malcolm was living while studying on a sabbatical at Stanford.

Malcolm's remarks were brief, beautiful, and so very true:

Nicky was an extraordinarily loveable and alive human being, with an illuminating goodness that seemed natural and innate. A good many years ago, one person wrote about him: "He is one of the most contributing, enthusiastic young people I know, liked by everyone, charming and active, always concerned about others." This simple, direct statement was more than a description of the moment, but rather a prophecy for the future. . . .

Nicky had joy in life in myriad ways—through his warmth and openness with people, through the sensitivity of his photography and poetry, through his love of sports and the outdoors, through his serenity and acceptance. His joy for life was reflected in the way he could put people at ease, in his infectious smile, in his animated discussions about skiing, in his exquisite pictures of sand and trees, or in his befriending a nondescript and unwanted dog who became his constant companion. . . .

And so, we are staggered and saddened by the loss of Nicky—and yet—through it we see more clearly his love of life expressed through his vitality and sense of caring; and we realize, in spite of our sorrow, that in truth "He has outsoared the shadow of our night."

One of the many things that touched me that weekend was the presence of four young men with whom Nick had made a summer-long canoe trip two years before. The trip was on the East Main River near the Arctic Circle. These were not local friends but friends Nick had made at college and at a Canadian canoe camp, yet four of the five flew in from points all around the country to attend the memorial service, proving how close the group had become and how much they thought of Nick. All four joined Nick's Wilmington friends as ushers.

Within weeks of Nick's death, we faced a troubling decision: Should we cancel our vacation plans?

Along with Rich and Blair Both, two of our closest friends, we had been eagerly looking forward to a very special and carefully planned vacation—two weeks on a rented houseboat on the Canal de Midi in Southern France. No, we said at first, it would be inappropriate to take such a pleasure trip in light of what had happened to our son. But, as others urged, it could be just what we needed. We decided to go. After all, not going would not bring Nicky back.

In spite of the awareness of tragedy, the trip was tremendously therapeutic, thanks in equal parts to the tranquil environment and the ministrations of our friends. We weren't sorry we decided to go.

But then it was summer, and time to face life again. Jeanne had trouble adjusting at first. As she later told Donna Joy Newman of the *Chicago Tribune,* "I kind of tuned out because it was such a publicly-oriented tragedy. I don't remember a great deal about that whole summer." To this day, she cannot recall the events of Watergate.

As for me, I found that I was increasingly haunted by the need to do what Jeanne would eventually say (in *Newsweek*), "to give a meaning to this vicious, senseless death."

I went back to work, but my mind was not totally on my job. A good-sized corner of it remained preoccupied with what I had come to call "the issue"—gun control. (Later, I would sharpen the focus to handguns, but at the time I was only beginning to learn about the issue.)

The inarticulateness that had plagued me when I first stood up in front of the press in San Francisco had given way to a growing curiosity about how something like this could happen. I started reading everything I could get my hands on. In June or July, I visited my congressman, Pete du Pont (now Delaware's governor), who had the Library of Congress send me some literature, all of which further stimulated my interest. I could not understand how a nation so concerned with law and order could at the same time allow small weapons of death and violence to move unchecked on its streets.

If a pamphlet mentioned other sources, I sent for them and read them with care, jotting down their main points for future study—and use in a document, a personal "White Paper" on gun control, that I was compiling. My intention was to teach myself about "the issue" by listing all the arguments, pro and con. Soon our down-stairs recreation room came to resemble a small office. Indeed, it looked like a branch office, but the trouble was that I didn't know what it was a branch office *of.* And that of course was part of the problem.

Thanksgiving was a difficult holiday that year. After some lengthy discussion, Jeanne and I decided to get away from Wilmington for a few days and went skiing. On the way back we stopped in the Scranton, Pennsylvania, area to visit friends of many years. While talking with them, I mentioned that as a result of Nick's death I was becoming increasingly interested in the subject of gun control. Not long after we got back home, they sent us a letter telling us of a strange coincidence.

Shortly after our visit, they heard from another old friend, a man named Ed Welles, who had just retired from the CIA. He told them that he was now spending his days in the service of a new lobbying organization in Washington, a small, underfinanced and understaffed *handgun control* lobby!

And that was how I came to meet Mark Borinsky, Ed Welles, and the National Council to Control Handguns (NCCH), the organization that has since become Handgun Control, Inc., the organization I am proud to represent as chairman. But that is getting ahead of the story.

Mark Borinsky, the founder of NCCH, had been motivated to do so by a very personal experience. He had been robbed and almost killed at gunpoint. A graduate student at the University of Chicago in the early 1970's, Mark and a friend were walking back toward campus one night about 9:30 when three young men jumped them. One had a handgun, or at least Mark and his friend believed he did, because he kept urging, "Let's shoot 'em!" After taking their money and their shoes—so the two victims couldn't follow them—the trio ran off, leaving two very shaken young men.

As Mark recalls: "When you're young, you think you will live forever, that you're invulnerable. But that encounter robbed me of that feeling. In a way, I think that's what the explosion in crime has done to the entire country. I was forced to realize that I could be dead, that my life could be ended at the whim of some punk!" He decided that when he finished school, he would find some way to fight the crime problem.

When Mark arrived in Washington a year or so later, his Ph.D. in psychology finished and his new job starting, he figured that he could join a gun control lobby and do *something* to help. He was sure he would find any number of organizations he could join, groups he thought would have sprung up naturally after the assassination of President Kennedy, the killing of Dr. King, and the murder of Robert Kennedy, plus the paralyzing of George Wallace—to mention only the most newsworthy shootings. Instead, he found nothing that resembled an effective anti-gun lobby.

So he did something about it himself. He set up the National Council to Control Handguns.

Using his own money, which he lent the organization, he rented a tiny office, found a secretary, and corralled a few like-minded people to serve as his incorporating officers and his board of directors. Then he put an ad in a neighborhood paper—not the *Washington Post* or *Star*—for a *volunteer* to be the day-to-day, on-the-scene head. As Mark had a job, he could not do both. The man who answered the ad was Ed Welles, recently retired from the CIA. It may have looked like a marriage of opposites, but it worked.

And that was the organization, such as it was, when I came down to Washington to meet Ed Welles in early 1975.

As it happened, there were gun control hearings going on at that very time in the House of Representatives. Ed was monitoring the hearings as an interested party, and he took me along with him. It was my baptism in congressional committee hearings.

Before very long I was a disciple. My education, which would be an ongoing process, had officially started. I began to take my vacation in single days so that I could be in Washington every Wednesday or Thursday, depending on which day the hearing on the handgun control bill was set for. In my spare time back home I worked on a letter which I eventually sent to friends asking for money for NCCH.

In May 1975, facing the obvious fact that work on "the issue" was becoming my main effort, my main involvement, I asked for a year's leave of absence without pay from Du Pont.

(Interestingly, unlike all other such requests that I had heard of in my twenty-six years with Du Pont, mine went up through the entire hierarchy of the company before it was approved. Although Du Pont does not make guns, it does own Remington Arms. In fairness to the company, I should point out that to my knowledge my leave request was the first of its type Du Pont had ever granted —for an executive to go to Washington and join a lobby. The company could simply have said no, told me I would have to resign. But it did not, and therefore, at least in theory, a job would be waiting for me at the end of the year—after I, as I'm sure some of my co-workers were thinking, "came to my senses.")

At the end of the twelve-month-period I extended the leave for six more months. When that time was up, I knew the direction of my immediate future. Before I made the final decision to leave Du Pont and work fulltime for handgun control, Jeanne and I sat down with our three children and asked them if they thought I was doing the right thing, because Nick's murder would obviously become even more public in the process.

"Okay," they said finally. I had their permission, and blessing, to use Nick's name—as long as I didn't get "maudlin or icky" about it.

At the end of 1976 I took formal early retirement from the Du Pont Company. Ever since then I have been associated with the organization now called Handgun Control, Inc., first as executive director and since 1978 as chairman, working to reduce this country's senseless level of handgun violence.

1
THE BODY COUNT

I was a rather unlikely convert to the crusade against handgun violence. Thanks mainly to the NRA (National Rifle Association) and its public positions, we tend to think of pro-gun people as being conservative, both socially and politically, and usually Republicans, whereas, according to the stereotype, anti-gun people are probably liberals, somewhat anti-establishment, and most likely Democrats.

Yet, even though I became a spokesman for handgun control, I fit more easily into the first group.

My father was a dentist with an office in Manhattan, but I was raised in the suburbs of Westchester County, New York, and later in Connecticut. I went to Yale, was a navy pilot in World War II, and took a job with the Du Pont Company in 1949. They sent me to Clinton, Iowa, where I spent several years before being called back to Wilmington, Delaware, the company's headquarters, where I've lived ever since. Like my father, I have been a registered Republican all my life.

What's more, I am a hunter. I enjoy duck and goose shooting on Chesapeake Bay and, when I get a chance, quail and pheasant shooting. I still have several shotguns in my house. In short, I don't fit the stereotype very well.

But that's one of the characteristics of handgun violence: it pays no attention to stereotypes or odds; it touches anyone, and therefore everyone. It may touch some groups of people more often than others, but there are no groups that are totally safe from it. Handgun violence is like a disease that is out there—waiting. You don't know when you might come in contact with it. And there's no pill that you can take to guard against it.

Prior to the death of our son, if I had been approached by a pollster and asked my position on handgun control, I would probably have said that I could see the logic of some form of licensing and control of handguns. But it was not a subject I had thought about a great deal or read about in depth. Like millions of other Americans, then and now, I had little personal motivation to do anything about a problem I unknowingly categorized as someone else's—because nothing had happened to me or to mine.

Because I wasn't a member of the NRA, I was not "sensitized" to their view of things by innumerable mailings warning me about the evils of gun control. Nick's death, of course, changed all that.

I was now a *victim* of handgun violence. And so were my wife Jeanne and our children Pam, David, and Leslie. Truly, anyone who had known Nick Shields was victimized by his death. His shooting made victims of an ever-widening circle of people, including his grandparents, his aunts and uncles, his friends, his former teachers and coaches. So many people, so many victims.

One loses so much when one loses a child. What might he have done with all those years he should have had? Might he even have done something great, something that would have benefited mankind? No one knows. No one can say. It is so terribly true, as I would hear too many times in the years following Nick's death, that when you lose a parent you lose your past, but when you lose a child, you lose part of your future.

Almost all of us have experienced the death of a loved one, either because of accident, disease, or simply old age. Natural death, while nonetheless sad, is something we can usually deal with in time. But violent death, such as in a car accident or because of a particularly virulent disease, invariably leaves us asking *why?* That terrible question seldom, if ever, yields a satisfactory answer.

But the most awful point about handgun deaths—whether we are talking about murder, suicide, or accidental shooting, all of what we might call "conspicuously caused violent deaths"—is that there *is* something we could have done about it. If we had, perhaps *some* of those lives would have been spared.

This is what I was coming to see as I began to read more and more about gun control and handgun control specifically.

As a businessman, I had been used to a certain amount of discipline in dealing with a problem, and as I read and studied, I became increasingly alarmed at the lack of discipline in regard to the problem of handgun violence, indeed, in regard to the problem of violence in America generally.

I learned that in less than ten years there had been *five* presidential commissions on the subject of violence. And every one reported that the situation was in fact grave. Yet it appeared that both the findings and the recommendations of these blue-ribbon commissions were being ignored.

The commissions were: 1. The Commission on Law Enforcement and Administration of Justice (1965); 2. The National Advisory Commission on Civil Disorders (1967), often referred to as "the Kerner Commission" because its chairman was Otto Kerner, then governor of Illinois; 3. The National Commission on the Causes and Prevention of Violence (1968), or "the Eisenhower Commission" after its head, Dr. Milton Eisenhower; 4. The National Commission on the Reform of Federal Criminal Laws; and, 5. The National Commission on Criminal Justice Standards and Goals (1971), known as the "Peterson Commission," after its chairman, Russell W. Peterson.

All five presidential commissions called for strict handgun controls, several even recommending a ban on the manufacture, sale, and possession of handguns.

I had not been studying the issue of gun control for long when I realized there were two fundamental observations to be made. And everything I have learned since then has only served to strengthen that realization. Those observations are:

One, the lack of effective controls over easily concealable handguns in America *defies common sense.*

Two, given the number of victims involved and the ongoing level of violence, what we have here is a *war,* an American Handgun War.

In the months following Nick's death, I pored over the literature on American violence. I read the reports of the presidential commissions, I read congressional testimony, plus books, magazines, and a sea of newspaper clippings. What I was trying to do, initially, was to find out if the situation was as bad as certain people said it was. What I soon learned was that it was not as bad —it was worse.

I learned that 1974, the year our son was killed, was the most violent year in American history. (As it turned out, it was the year in which handgun violence in America "peaked," at least for a few years; since 1979, we have exceeded the '74 figures and are now climbing toward a new and even more horrible peak.)

In 1974, there were 20,600 murders in the United States, and of that number 54 percent, or *11,124*, were handgun murders. That's Nick Shields and 11,123 *other* Americans! And all of them left behind loved ones.

In addition to the handgun murders, in 1974 there were also 14,345 suicides and 2,513 accidental deaths by firearms or explosives. Of the suicides, it is safe to assume that over 90 percent were by firearms of all types, and over 50 percent by handguns. Of the accidental deaths, again it is safe to assume that over 50 percent were by handguns.

I was startled to learn that, according to FBI figures, the national homicide rate (per 100,000 population) doubled between 1964 and 1974. And, during the same period, the handgun homicide rate nearly *tripled.* One figure that struck me was that, according to a study made in 1974 by the Massachusetts Institute of Technology, a child born and living in Atlanta would have a one in twenty-five chance of being murdered; one in thirty-six for a child born in Washington, D.C.; and in New York City one chance in sixty.

Although most of my early reading had to do with the nature and size of the violence problem in America, I did occasionally read comparative studies. One fact I ran across was particularly unsettling: In 1974, the year Nick was killed, the year in which 11,124 Americans were murdered with handguns, in the nation of Japan, which has half our population, there were only thirty-seven handgun murders in the entire country! (See Chapter 4, "World Opinion, World Law," for more on this point.)

These figures, however, were only the figures for deaths. There was a horrendous amount of other violence at large in our society that year, and handguns continued to play a major role.

In 1974 there were 441,290 robberies, and a gun was used in an estimated 45 percent of them. There were also 452,720 cases of aggravated assault, and a gun figured in one out of four. (These figures represent all guns, but it is safe to say that the great majority of them were handguns.)

As for rape, that year the FBI reported that there was an estimated total of 55,210 forcible rapes, which was an increase of 8 percent over the previous year, and represented about 6 percent of all the violent crimes in 1974. It should be noted, however, that many rapes go unreported in our society for a number of reasons, not the least of which is the ordeal the reporting process imposes upon the victim.

This is probably a good place to point out that in regard to reported crime one has to be extremely careful about the figures used. About the only thing that can be said without fear of contradiction is that no one knows the *exact* figures for anything. Recognized experts disagree not only on the number of handguns in circulation, but on the incidence of violent crime.

The difficulty of getting accurate figures does not mean that the true picture of violence is actually better than the one painted by the media. It is every bit as bad, and for all we know even worse.

Consider this: In 1974, there were approximately 250,000 Americans victimized with handguns. That is as if the entire population were being held at gunpoint in a *city* the size of:

Sacramento, California
Des Moines, Iowa
Richmond, Virginia, or
St. Petersburg, Florida.

Another thing I learned quite early is how terribly prominent a part the handgun has played in the history of assassinations in this country. In all but one of the thirteen assassinations and attempted assassinations of Presidents or presidential candidates, the assassin used a handgun. Presidents Lincoln, Garfield, and McKinley were slain. Candidate Robert Kennedy was killed. Candidate George Wallace was crippled.

The complete list also includes: Andrew Jackson, 1835, attempt;

former President Theodore Roosevelt, 1912, wounded; Franklin Roosevelt, 1933, attempt; Harry Truman, 1950, attempt; John Kennedy, 1963, killed; Gerald Ford, 1975, two attempts; and Ronald Reagan, 1981, wounded.

Both Lincoln and Garfield were killed with .44-caliber pistols, McKinley with a .32; the gun used to shoot Ronald Reagan was a .22 caliber revolver.

And in 1975, as I was beginning to spend more and more of my time in Washington learning about the handgun issue, in the month of September alone there were *two* attempts on the life of President Ford, both by would-be assassins using handguns.

Any reasonable person, seeing the statistics and the history of handgun violence, has to wonder what this is doing—what this has done—to the quality of our national life. How much of the highly publicized flight to the suburbs in the late '60's and early '70's was due to the quite justified fear of crime in the cities? And, in the '80's, with reports of crime waves in *rural* areas, how many people now say they are afraid to walk the streets of their cities and towns?

Do I exaggerate? Is it possible that 1974 was unusually violent and that the picture today is not as bad? Look at the statistics for 1979, the most recent year for which they are available:

10,728 handgun murders (out of a total of 21,456 murders)—
    up almost 12 percent over the previous year
75,989 rapes—up 13.2 percent
466,881 robberies (40 percent of which involved a gun)—up
    12 percent
614,213 aggravated assaults—up 10.1 percent

As for 1980, preliminary FBI figures indicate another across-the-board increase of about 10 percent.

Again, let me stress that these are just the *reported* figures. The actual figures are undoubtedly higher, and perhaps *much* higher. When individuals are questioned in a random sampling, the number of crimes that go *unreported* appears to be at least equal to the number reported, so the incidence of actual crime is probably twice the official statistics. Is it any wonder that while some people do not yet believe that they may be killed by a handgun, many

Americans now believe that in their lifetime they may be *threatened* by one?

Following the killing of Dr. Martin Luther King Jr., Robert Kennedy said:

> "The victims of the violence are black and white, rich and poor, young and old, famous and unknown. They are, most important of all, human beings whom other human beings loved and needed. No one—no matter where he lives or what he does—can be certain who next will suffer from some senseless act of bloodshed. And yet it goes on and on and on in this country of ours. Why?"

One reads Bobby Kennedy's words with a twinge, knowing that only weeks later he too would be one of the "famous" victims. But a more recent example is every bit as sad and ironic.

In early November 1980, at a dinner party in Washington, I met a medical doctor by the name of Michael Halberstam. When he learned that I was involved in the fight for handgun controls he became very interested. He was a bright and vital man who was also a journalist and an author. At the end of the evening he said he'd like to read some of our literature. A few days later I took it to him. To my surprise, because he had not mentioned his intention, a week or so later, on November 21, Michael Halberstam did a commentary on the cable news television network on handgun control.

After three paragraphs that were highly flattering to me, he said:

> Pete Shields needs everybody's support. Each year, 20,000 Americans are killed by handguns, compared to 100 or 200 who die by highly publicized illnesses like multiple sclerosis and muscular dystrophy.
>
> Let's start to put some of the same energy and urgency into controlling handguns as we put into controlling muscular dystrophy. Start now. Don't wait until someone you love and someone you respect has been murdered by a psychopath with a grudge against society and a .32 special in his pocket.

On Friday, December 5, Michael Halberstam and his wife, Elliott, came home to have a quick snack before seeing a movie. He surprised a burglar and was shot and killed—by a .32.

Later, we learned that Dr. Halberstam had made another commentary that day. It reads:

> I'm not one of those doctors who's always warning his patients not to take chances. I think that one reason for this is that I rather like to take chances myself. I'd rather ski downhill than cross-country. I like football rather than Frisbee. I still prefer baseball to softball.
>
> But I want to take *my* chances, not someone else's. That's why I'm in favor of handgun control. Not *banning* handguns but licensing and registering them, keeping them out of the hands of criminals and psychopaths.
>
> Each year in this country, 20,000 Americans are killed by handguns. Half of them are suicides, but the rest accidents and murders.
>
> I don't want to be the guy shot when I honk at the guy next to me and he reaches in his glove compartment and starts blasting away. I don't want my son shot when some punk holds up the filling station where he works, panics, and starts shooting.
>
> Handgun control has nothing to do with banning handguns, but, altogether, it has to do with keeping them under control and registered. That has nothing to do with hunting. We're going to keep hunting in this country. It has everything to do with the national epidemic of sudden, violent, foolish deaths.
>
> It may be true that guns don't kill and people do, but handguns make it a lot easier. Too easy.

Everyone who knew Michael Halberstam was shaken by the terrible, senseless killing that he himself had almost predicted. But we, and the nation and world, were in for another massive shock only a few days later.

On Monday, December 8, outside the Dakota apartment building in New York City, former Beatle John Lennon—who had become a social and cultural hero especially for the young, and who preached that we should "give peace a chance"—was killed with a handgun.

And then, less than four months later, a young man who wanted to prove his love for a teenage movie star by killing the President of the United States, shot at and *almost* killed Ronald Reagan.

As Robert Kennedy said, the bloodshed goes on and on and on, and the victims of handgun violence represent the entire spectrum of Americans, the famous and the unknown.

Kennedy. King. Kennedy. Lennon. And almost Reagan. Those are the famous. Here are the names of *some* of the not-so-famous, the unknowns, also killed on the battlefields of America.

DECEMBER 8, 1980, THE DAY JOHN LENNON WAS SHOT:

Houston, Texas: Teresa Handy, eighteen, was pronounced dead on arrival at Ben Taub Hospital. She had been shot in the chest with a .357-caliber revolver.

Natchez, Mississippi: William Heathcoat, twenty-seven, accidentally killed himself with a revolver, apparently playing the game of Russian Roulette.

Hilo, Hawaii: John Kahalewai, sixteen, was shot in the chest and killed with a handgun.

Washington, D.C.: John Bowen, thirty, was shot to death when he exchanged gunfire with a bank robber. Bowen, a bank customer, tried to foil the holdup of a downtown Washington bank.

San Antonio, Texas: Roberto Rangel, seventeen, was fatally shot by a hitchhiker.

Washington, D.C.: Louis Shorter, nineteen, died from a gunshot he suffered during a fight on the playground of Hine Junior High School.

Caesar, Mississippi: W.E. Summers was shot and killed with a handgun. A .32-caliber pistol, reportedly purchased earlier in the day in Picayune, was found near the body.

Chicago, Illinois: Sherwood Montgomery, twenty-four, was shot to death by a stranger on the West Side of Chicago.

MARCH 30, 1981, THE DAY PRESIDENT REAGAN WAS SHOT:

Dallas, Texas: Officer T. J. McCarthy, twenty-four, was shot in the head with a .32-caliber revolver while on a routine patrol.

Akron, Ohio: Edward Highley, twenty-one, was shot in the chest and head with a small-caliber handgun while working at a local gas station.

Baltimore, Maryland: Dr. Sebastian Russo, fifty-seven, was shot in the chest with a handgun during an apparent robbery attempt at his office.

San Francisco, California: Winfred McGee, thirty-six, a

twelve-year municipal railway bus driver, was shot to
death with a .38-caliber automatic pistol.

In the days immediately following the attempt on the President's life, Handgun Control, Inc. took out full-page ads in major newspapers throughout the country. At the top of the page, we wrote: "THE DAY THE PRESIDENT WAS SHOT WAS AN AVERAGE KIND OF DAY." It was an average kind of day because approximately 50 Americans were killed by handguns that day. 50 handgun deaths. Included in that 50 could have been you, or me, or anyone. Think about it.

Every month, Handgun Control, Inc. puts out a newsletter called "The Handgun Body Count," which lists the names of handgun victims reported killed in each of the fifty states. In addition to reminding people that each one of these statistics was a real person with a *name*, the title of the newsletter is an intentional reference to the daily body counts of the Vietnam War. We hope that the title will evoke grim memories of that war and the nightly news accounts—especially the televised ones—of the carnage. It was in part as a result of those constant announcements of American lives lost that the public rose up, finally, in opposition to that war. And now we have another war we must rise up and stop— the American Handgun War.

Here are some names selected from a recent issue of the "Handgun Body Count." All of these victims of handguns were *children*.

Chicago, Illinois: Limari Castro, one-year-old, was killed in
her crib when a neighbor's .357 Magnum revolver
accidentally fired in the apartment above her family's and
penetrated the ceiling.
Washington, D.C.: Derrick Johnson, nine, was shot and killed
by his four-year-old cousin who was playing with his
father's .38-caliber revolver.
Monterey, California: Marcus Reed, nine, was shot in the
head and killed by a ten-year-old friend who was playing
with his parents' .357 Magnum handgun.
Champaign, Illinois: Nikieta Emory, two, was accidentally
shot in the head and killed by her four-year-old brother

after he found a .22-caliber handgun, kept for protection,
in a dresser drawer.

Chicago, Illinois: Marcella Baker, one-year-old, was shot in
the head and killed when a .38-caliber handgun her sister
was playing with discharged. The gun was bought for
protection.

The NRA says, "Guns don't kill, people do." Who will explain
that to these children?

The number of Americans we said are killed by handguns every
day—fifty—is a very conservative figure which includes those
killed by accident and those who take their own lives. The average
figure for those who are *murdered* by handguns every day in the
United States, day in and day out, month after month and year
after year, is twenty-nine. *Twenty-nine!*

Until Americans get sufficiently angry—righteously angry—
nothing will be done to control handguns. So we at Handgun
Control, Inc. are trying to make people see that what is happening
on our streets today is nothing short of war. Indeed, *all* of our
publications now use the phrase "the American Handgun War."

In case anyone thinks this is going too far, consider the following: During the seven peak years of the Vietnam War (1966–72)
42,300 American soldiers were killed in combat; during that same
period, the number of Americans murdered with handguns on the
streets of this country was over 52,000!

Are we wrong to call the uncontrolled handgun situation a
"war"? A film put out by Handgun Control opens with dramatiza-
tions of several ordinary citizens being shot or threatened with
handguns. The narrator speaks as follows:

"This is not Vietnam—not World War II. It's America—our home—
yet our people are dying daily in our streets as if they were on
some foreign battlefield. Day after day, month after month, year
after bloody year . . . it continues and escalates at such a staggering
pace that we can no longer go about our daily lives unthreatened.
We try to put the handgun problem out of our minds. We want to
believe those tragedies only happen to somebody else. And
although we can feel sympathy for the victims, we cannot feel the
pain. But, in all likelihood, you'll get your chance.

"As each day passes, the probability increases that *it is* going to happen to you . . . or to somebody you're close to.

"This is not an idle threat. It's a fact!

"At the present rate of occurrence, there is a one-in-five chance that you or a member of your family will be attacked or threatened by someone with a handgun.

"Now think about *that!*

"Think about that tonight, as you're going to your car, or waiting for the bus, or walking the dog, or doing hundreds of things you do in your normal daily routine. Think about it . . . and think about your one-in-five chance, and then think if that's the kind of life you want or the kind of life you want for your family.

"That's why we call this a war!"

The crucial point is: Until you understand that *you* could be the next casualty in the American Handgun War, you do not understand the problem.

2
THE HANDGUN COUNT

DEPENDING on whose figures you use, there are anywhere from 40 to 60 million handguns in circulation in America today. Here is the story of one of them. It happens to be the gun that killed my son.

The Zebra killers in San Francisco were responsible for fifteen murders, seven attempted murders, and one rape. Of the fifteen people killed, the first was hacked to death with a machete and the remaining fourteen were shot with a .32-caliber Beretta, a semi-automatic pistol made in Italy.

The murder weapon had to be found to complete a chain of evidence connecting the suspects to the killings. But there was a problem. The first seven had been killed with one .32-caliber Beretta and the remaining seven with a *different* gun of the same make and caliber. When they learned that the criminals had switched guns, the inspectors in charge of the investigation were extremely worried. Did this mean the killers had already disposed of the first gun and, if so, might they not do the same thing with the second gun, and then perhaps even with a third or fourth? If they did, the chances of catching and convicting any of them would be slim.

Then the second gun was found—by two children playing in the backyard of a home less than two blocks from where Nick was shot. Ballistics tests showed it to be the weapon used to kill the last seven victims. The serial number of the weapon—A47469—was fed into the state police computer, which had no record of it. The police then contacted the local agent of the Treasury Department's Bureau of Alcohol, Tobacco and Firearms. The job of tying the handgun to the killers had begun.

The twists and turns and seeming dead-ends that followed are in many ways typical of a handgun's history in this country, especially a small, concealable gun that has no other purpose but the killing of humans.

The ATF has a handgun tracing service, established in October 1972. According to a former ATF official, ATF agents, "by telephone or telegraph, transmit to the tracing center in Washington a description of the gun involved. The initial job of the tracer is to determine the manufacturer, who is then contacted by telephone. The manufacturers—both domestic and foreign—advise the tracer to whom the gun was consigned when it was shipped from the factory. Our tracers follow the path of the gun to its first retail sale."

The ATF returned the information that the Beretta—model 70, 7.65-millimeter, which is the same as a .32-caliber semi-automatic pistol, blue steel, with a 3″ barrel—had been made by the Pietro Beretta Company of Gardone, Italy, and shipped to J.L. Galef & Son, an American firearms importer in New York, in April 1968. It was sold on May 22 of that year to the J.C. Penney Company's purchasing outlet in North Carolina, which shipped it to a Penney store in Takoma, Washington, on June 7th. Seven weeks later, on July 31, 1968, the gun was bought by a man who lived in that area.

The ATF agent in charge of the search was disheartened to learn that the gun was six years old. That would probably mean, he figured, that the gun would have passed through a number of hands. He was right.

In 1974, the initial buyer no longer lived in Takoma, so the agent checked to see if he had a California driver's license and found that he had. The address, in Santa Barbara, was that of the man's mother, who told the agent her son now lived in a religious commune about fifty miles outside San Francisco. Found there, the man was helpful. He said he had sold the gun (which he had bought "on impulse" and never even fired) to his roommate, a man named Brad Bishop.

Bishop turned out to be considerably harder to find. A felon previously arrested on drug-related charges, he was known to be traveling under the alias of James A. Wilson. The agent then located Bishop's mother, in Marin County, and she said she thought he was working for a construction company south of Los Angeles. When that lead proved fruitless, the agents questioned over two dozen of Bishop's friends and acquaintances, and when one mentioned that he had sold him a station wagon, the ATF put out the information to all law-enforcement points in the state. Almost immediately, Santa Monica police reported that the car had recently been abandoned there.

By this time, based largely on the testimony of an informant, there were four suspects in the Zebra killings. They had been indicted and trial was set for July 1974. The police were under extreme pressure to trace the Beretta back to at least one of them or one of their close associates.

The police then arranged to have Bishop's picture shown on television and asked for help in locating him, although because of legal restrictions they could not say it was in connection with the Zebra case. However, Bishop's mother became alarmed by the publicity and called the police with the names of several more people who might know where he was. One of those leads said Bishop had gone to Honolulu.

After a long and complicated search, the police and the ATF agent found Bishop on the island of Maui, where they questioned him. He said he'd sold the handgun for $20, not long after buying it from the original purchaser, to a man named St. Andre, who told Bishop a week later that someone had stolen it. Both Bishop and St. Andre knew who had stolen it, so they confronted the thief, and got him to pay them $75 for the gun. Since this had all taken place in San Francisco, the police there were able to continue the investigation without further ATF help.

The police found the gun thief in San Bruno, and he told them he'd sold the gun, after having it for only three days, to a druggist in San Francisco, who in turn said he had also kept it only a short time, selling it for $80 to "a middle-aged Samoan known only as 'Moo Moo.'"

When he was found, Moo Moo insisted that he had pawned the gun—in May 1973, at the San Francisco Loan Association—for

$25, reclaimed it at the end of August, and then, because he was "nervous" carrying it, thrown it into a trash basket only three blocks from the pawnshop.

Although they felt the Samoan was lying, the police interviewed all the trashmen who worked that neighborhood, but to no avail. Then, just as they were about to visit Moo Moo again and press him, they received word that he had been admitted to the San Francisco morgue, dead of a massive heart attack.

The police were devastated, though they had one consolation: The trial of the four men had been postponed until March 1975, giving them eight more months to trace the Beretta. Then they got a break.

One of the inspectors in charge of the case got a call that an informant of his, currently in jail, wanted to see him. Thinking it involved some minor matter, he postponed the meeting. When he got to the county jail several days later, the informant told him that he had sold a "lot of stuff" to a man who worked at Black Self-Help—which happened to be where several of the defendants had also worked.

When asked what kind of "stuff" he'd sold him, the inmate said that it was "stuff like refrigerators and guns. I sold him a .38 once, and a couple of Berettas."

The policeman asked where he got the Berettas. He said that he'd gotten one of them from "a big Samoan guy called Moo Moo." That name had never been in the papers or otherwise mentioned by the media and the policeman knew the man was telling the truth. The long trail had ended.

In 1976, the four men accused of being the Zebra killers were convicted of multiple murders. The verified presence of the Beretta A47469 at the place where they worked and met played a vital role in their conviction.

And that is the story of how just one handgun out of an estimated 40 to 60 million in the United States today tumbled from hand to hand for six years, going from solid citizen to murderous felon.

Here are the blunt facts on handguns in circulation in America:

—40 to 60 million now.
—2.5 million *more* produced and sold every year.

—At current rates, approximately 100 million in circulation by the year 2000.

—A new handgun sold every thirteen seconds.

—One in five Americans with access to a handgun.

Given these facts, is it any wonder that one of us is murdered with a handgun in the United States every fifty minutes?

Handguns come in all sizes, shapes, weights, and levels of quality. They are made and sold by the following U.S. companies:

U.S. PRODUCTION OF HANDGUNS
(nonmilitary) IN 1979*

Company	Pistols	Revolvers	Total	Percentage of Industry	Headquarters
Smith & Wesson	58,716	558,709	617,425	28.6	Springfield, Mass.
Sturm, Ruger & Company	66,516	312,088	378,604	17.6	Southport, Conn.
Colt Industries	95,100	115,897	210,997	9.8	Hartford, Conn.
Harrington & Richardson	—	180,344	180,344	8.4	Gardner, Mass.
R. G. Industries	17,476	157,267	174,743	8.1	Miami, Fla.
Raven Arms	79,165	—	79,165	3.7	Industry, Calif.
Charter Arms	—	67,259	67,259	3.1	Stratford, Conn.
Dan Wesson Arms	—	61,065	61,065	2.8	Monson, Mass.
Sterling Arms	59,985	—	59,985	2.8	Gasport, N. Y.
Firearms Import & Export	34,673	23,952	58,625	2.7	Opa Locka, Fla.
Thompson/ Center Arms	44,401	—	44,401	2.1	Rochester, N.Y.
Excam	37,314	—	37,314	1.7	Hialeah, Fla.
North American Arms	30,242	—	30,242	1.4	Provo, Utah
High Standard	27,510	2,117	29,627	1.4	East Hartford, Conn.
F.I. Industries	28,059	—	28,059	1.3	Accokeek, Md.
Bauer Firearms	21,302	—	21,302	1.0	Fraser, Mich.
All others	64,355	12,305	76,660	3.5	
Total	664,814	1,491,003	2,155,820	100.0	

*Source: Bureau of Alcohol, Tobacco and Firearms. Compiled by Handgun Control, Inc. in May 1981.

You can get a used handgun for $25 or $30 in an alley of any big city in this country, or you can pay up to hundreds of dollars in a brightly lighted, nicely appointed shop on Main Street. In either case there will be few if any embarrassing questions asked. Failing that, if you live in some cities you can take part in a new program called, unofficially, Rent-a-Handgun! (This program will most likely spread to other cities—until we get an effective *federal* handgun law.)

Each year, American companies manufacture or assemble well over two million handguns—and they do so largely free of federal controls.

The word "assemble" represents an important distinction. In 1968, in the rush of anger and guilt which followed the killings of Dr. Martin Luther King and Senator Robert Kennedy, the Congress of the United States passed a bill that tried to limit the supply of certain handguns. The Gun Control Act of 1968 banned the importation "non-sporting handguns," or what are commonly referred to as "Saturday Night Specials," but it left a large loophole, as it turned out, by not banning the importation of the *parts* that, once assembled, comprise such guns.

The gun that John Hinckley, Jr., bought at Rocky's Pawnshop in Dallas and carried with him to Washington to shoot President Reagan was an assembled gun. As reported in the *Washington Post:*

> The gun that shot Ronald Reagan yesterday was manufactured months ago, thousands of miles away from the nation's capital in a small factory in Germany. The .22-caliber, blue steel revolver was then shipped in pieces to Miami, where it was assembled, thus skirting U.S. laws that make it illegal to import small, inexpensive foreign-made handguns. The Roehm model, RG14 handgun is no stranger to American soil. The revolver is one of the best known handguns in this country, say gun experts and police. It is best known as a Saturday Night Special—the type of handgun that Congress thought it was getting rid of when it passed the national Gun Control Act of 1968.
>
> . . . The gun that shot the 40th President was assembled at a Miami factory, one of 15,000 to 20,000 cheap revolvers that roll off its assembly line each month . . . Identified by sources as the gun confiscated by the Secret Service after Reagan, press aide James

Brady and two law-enforcement officers were shot, the Roehm
revolver is a six-shot, double-action, 15-ounce revolver that can fire
any .22 caliber ammunition. Its parts are shipped to R.G. Industries
at 2485 Northwest 20th Street, Miami, for assembly . . . R.G.
Industries was formed by the German-based Roehm family after the
1968 Gun Control Act was passed. The company's primary product
is cheap handguns, and it employs up to 80 assembly-line workers.
Last year, R.G. Industries sold an estimated $3.1 million worth of
handguns . . .

So, despite the 1968 Gun Control Act, foreign-made handguns
of all types and sizes keep flowing in at the rate of more than 600
a day. These, plus American-made products, add up to almost
6,000 new handguns *per day*.

If the number of handguns in circulation in the United States
increased by more than 20 million in the 1970s, what then will
happen in the last two decades of this century? It is entirely possible that Handgun Control, Inc.'s estimate of 100 million handguns
in circulation in America by the year 2000 will turn out to be too
low. Unless, that is, something is done to stem the frightening rise
in the number of handguns on the streets of America.

The American handgun manufacturing industry is one of the
most secretive in the entire nation. Until 1972, the companies
were not required by the government to report how many handguns they made or assembled, and not until several years later
were they required to let anyone but themselves and the government know what those figures were—despite the fact that their
sole product was a small machine designed to do one thing: kill
human beings.

In 1976, the Police Foundation did a study of firearms abuse and
reported: "Nobody knows how many guns are being made, imported, or sold each year. The gun companies don't publish the
figures, and despite the obvious effect of guns on American life,
the government remains content to let the firearms industry conduct its business in secret. In a country that keeps public count on
almost everything else—from the sales of candy bars to the returns
on paperback books—the absence of statistics about guns consti-
tutes what might be called a violent anomaly." The Police Foundation study suggested that production figures might be obtained if
some interested party filed a Freedom of Information (FOI) suit.

That is exactly what Handgun Control, Inc. did. But even though we "won" the suit in an out-of-court settlement, we did not get all the information we had asked for. The government, mindful of the manufacturers' complaints that competitors would be able to learn their marketing strategies, agreed that it would release the figures but not until they were more than a year old. Thus we did not get the 1979 figures in the charts in Appendixes F and H until 1980-81.

As a businessman, I was a bit surprised to learn that the handgun industry markets its products just like any other business, despite the fact that the product is potentially deadly. A typical handgun moves from the factory to the street almost as if it were toothpaste or chewing gum. By paying a modest license fee, a manufacturer buys the right to produce and sell handguns. There are no restrictions on quantity, quality, or size. Beyond minimal recording and reporting requirements, little else is required to keep the license. The manufacturers sell the handguns to dealers, who pay only a $10 annual licensing fee to sell to the public.

For a private citizen to buy a gun, all that is required is the completion of a basic informational form that asks for little more than the purchaser's name, address, age, and whether he or she has a criminal record or any mental or drug-related problem. In many states neither the buyer's identity nor the truth of his answers is verified. We trust the buyer's word, hoping that he has told the truth.

There is no limit on the number of handguns one person may buy. Further, there are even fewer restrictions on resale.

As maddening as I, a businessman, found the marketing of handguns to be, I was infuriated by something uncovered, quite by chance, by Henry Bashkin, a retired government economist who is one of our volunteers. While wading through the Multilateral Trade Agreement of 1979, engineered for the U.S. by Robert Strauss, President Carter's Special Trade Representative, Henry discovered that the U.S. tariff on handgun *parts* (so many of which, when assembled, become Saturday Night Specials) which had been 21 percent, had been reduced to 8.4 percent. This *60 percent* reduction was the highest that could be granted, under the authorizations then in effect.

Under the old tariff, the manufacturer paid the U.S. Treasury $210,000 on every million dollars' worth of imported parts. Under the 8.4 percent tariff, that immediately dropped to $84,000—a loss to the government of $126,000. The money "saved"—or should we call it a *subsidy?*—was probably split between the manufacturer and his foreign supplier.

Not only was the glaring loophole in the 1968 Gun Control Act being cynically exploited by foreign and domestic manufacturers alike, they were now being rewarded for that exploitation with more profits—and this by an administration whose leader had run for the presidency on the promise that he would do something about the handgun problem. He did something about it—he made it worse!

We complained immediately to Strauss, and were told by his office that they had nothing to do with health and safety. Their only concern was "trade." We also complained on Capitol Hill, but while Congressman Vanik of Ohio did introduce a bill to deny the tariff reduction to gun parts, and held hearings, the measure never got out of committee. Therefore the reduced tariff remains.

The handgun industry takes no part in the debate over handgun control. It can probably depend on the NRA and other pro-pistol groups to preserve its profitability.

When, in 1968, Congress passed the Gun Control Act, which banned the importation of what it termed "non-sporting handguns" (Saturday Night Specials), it did not define them. To remedy this, a committee was formed to decide on the criteria which would be used to determine which handguns could and could not be brought into the country. Interestingly, the committee included representatives from the handgun industry (a fact that we learned only by filing another FOI suit) but none from the pro-control group that existed at that time. The fruits of the committee's labor—known as "Factoring Criteria for Weapons"—appears on page 50. It indicates how difficult it is to classify handguns.

Under the simplest definition, a handgun is a gun designed to be fired with one hand. All other firearms, when used properly and as designed, require the use of both hands (and arms).

Those of us in the handgun control movement have come to refer to the type of handgun most in need of regulation as an "easily concealable" handgun, because it is the ease of concealability that makes such a weapon the favorite of the criminal and therefore so dangerous. (It is also true that the accuracy of a pistol increases as the barrel length becomes greater, so one can see that

the small gun with the short barrel is not suitable for target shooting or any other form of handgun sport.) But the term is subject
to some misinterpretation for the simple reason that if you try
hard enough you can "conceal" almost any handgun. In general,
however, we are talking about a gun with a barrel of three inches
or less.

The most commonly used term for such a gun is "Saturday Night
Special." The term was coined in the Detroit area in the late
1950's and early '60's when, because of police crackdowns, it became harder to buy a handgun there, so residents in search of a
handgun drove an hour or so to Toledo, Ohio, where the handgun
laws were loose to nonexistent. The weapon they usually bought
was cheap, had a short barrel, and was of smaller caliber. So many
of these were used in crimes—particularly crimes of passion on
weekends—that the Detroit police labeled any handgun of this
type a Saturday Night Special.

The government arm charged with enforcing the provisions of
the 1968 Gun Control Act, the Treasury's Bureau of Alcohol, Tobacco, and Firearms, defines a Saturday Night Special this way:
". . . an inexpensive, concealable weapon that has become common in street crime usage . . . one which had a barrel length of
three inches or less, and one which was relatively inexpensive."

In general, handguns are distinguishable by their: 1. physical
size; 2. safety features (such as the presence of a "safety," which
is a device that prevents firing until a lever is moved); 3. caliber
(those up to .32-caliber are considered small, and those over that
large); and 4. quality (a top-of-the-line Smith & Wesson or Colt sells
for several hundred dollars).

Although expensive handguns are sometimes used in crime, the
real enemy in the American Handgun War remains the small,
cheap, easily concealable handgun—like the one used to shoot
President Reagan. R.G. Industries' list price for that gun is about
$45, but it often sells at retail for $10 to $15 less.

According to our most recent information, R.G. Industries,
which in 1977 had only 4 percent of the market, increased its
share to 8 percent in 1979, more than doubling its market.

*In other words, the company is selling more and more of the
kind of gun that almost killed the President, the kind of gun that
has only one purpose: to kill people.*

3
WHY DO PEOPLE
OWN HANDGUNS?

A NSWERS to the question "Why do people own or acquire *handguns?*" are entirely different from answers to the question "Why do people own rifles and shotguns?"

It is not at all difficult to explain why people own firearms other than handguns. From southern Florida to northern Michigan, and from Portland, Washington, to Portland, Maine, men and women have been using rifles and shotguns for hunting and for sport for as long as this country has been a country—and before. Their use of firearms—rifles and shotguns—is not part of the problem.

As Handgun Control, Inc. has *always* stressed, the American hunter and the American sportsman know how to use their guns. They are trained and they are careful. (Indeed, the NRA itself provides excellent training in the use of guns.)

The true hunter and sportsman knows that he is part of a long and proud tradition of responsible gun use in this country. He understands that he is in a sense the modern counterpart of those who shot for food or for sport when this country was young. He and his kind not only respect that tradition, they also respect the awesome killing power of their guns. A great number of them belong to the National *Rifle* Association. Many of them also belong to Handgun Control, Inc.

It is important to understand that our organization, Handgun

Control, Inc., does not propose further controls on rifles and shotguns. Rifles and shotguns are not the problem; they are not *concealable.*

Why do people own and acquire handguns? That's the hard question. There are many answers to it. Some are perfectly logical, others questionable, and a few downright hard to figure.

CRIMINAL ACTIVITY

After the handgun, the criminal's next weapon of choice is the knife, but it is such a far second that guns used in crime outnumber knives used in crime by *at least* three to one. The handgun, especially one with a relatively short barrel, is the preferred weapon of crime because it is both so lethal and so easily concealed. Stuck inside the belt, only the grip or handle is visible, and a jacket or suitcoat or sweater can easily cover that small bulge. Also, the handgun slips easily into a coat, jacket pocket or purse. The inside of an automobile offers any number of handy hiding spots. One glance at the illustrations of the short-barrel handgun on pages 50 and 51 is enough to show how easy it is to conceal a small handgun.

In the American Handgun War, the small, easily concealable handgun in the wrong hands is the *enemy.* For despite what the pro-pistol lobby says, guns *do* kill people. One person every fifty minutes.

SELF-DEFENSE

The frightening rise in crimes of violence throughout the country has caused more and more well-intentioned people to arm themselves. They buy guns to protect their homes and to carry with them for personal protection when traveling. Many, many people now carry handguns in their cars. Perhaps we should not have been so startled by an incident at the height of the gasoline crisis a few years ago, when one motorist shot and killed another who had cut in front of him in a filling-station line.

Unfortunately, instead of protection, what the new handgun

owner too often gets is personal tragedy. As I found out in my original reading, and as research in the area of self-defense has borne out ever since, a handgun does not protect the American home very well.

The home handgun is far more likely to kill or injure family members and friends than anyone who breaks in, and is especially harmful to young adults and to children.

Because 90 percent of burglaries take place when no one is home, the handgun bought for self-defense is very often stolen. According to law-enforcement authorities, each year an estimated 100,000 handguns are stolen from law-abiding citizens. These guns then enter the criminal underworld and are used in more crimes. Thus, inadvertently, the solid citizen is helping to arm the criminal class.

As a New York City police sergeant recently pointed out to a homeowner who asked if he should buy a handgun to protect his home, too often it is the homeowner *himself* who ends up getting shot and killed, because he most often *warns* the robber by saying something like "Stop!" or "What do you think you're doing?" Alerted, the thief turns and fires.

Another reason the handgun is not essential for home protection is that citizens in their homes don't need the one feature which most appeals to and attracts the criminal to the handgun—its concealability. The shotgun is far more intimidating to the intruder.

In street crime, the use of a handgun for self-defense is extremely risky, with the defender often losing the weapon and having it used against him. The handgun owner seldom even gets the *chance* to use his or her weapon because the element of surprise is always with the attacker. In fact, trying to use a handgun to ward off someone bent on aggravated assault makes the risk of death quite a bit higher.

For the ordinary citizen, using a handgun is seldom helpful for self-defense on the street. And, in the home, about the only way to get real protection from a personal handgun would be to have it always at the ready, perhaps in hand every time there is a knock on the door, loaded and ready to fire. That is not exactly the American way. Or my idea of a civilized society.

One question should be asked of anyone who says he or she

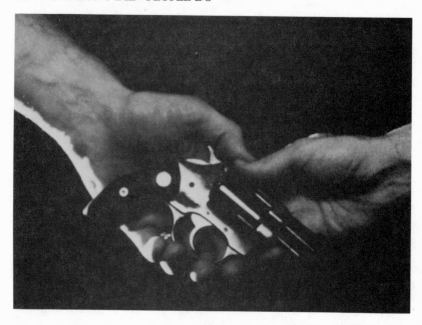

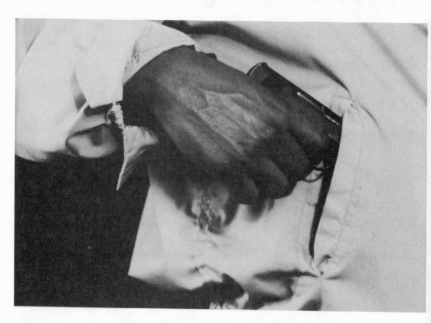

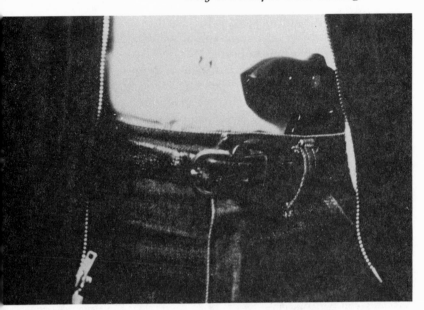

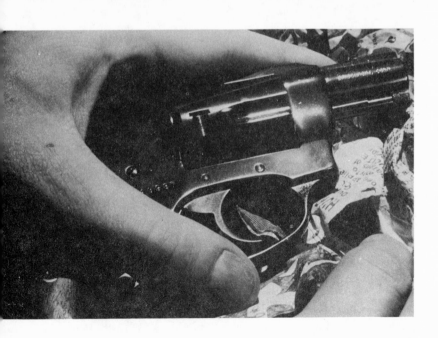

would be willing to use a handgun to keep from being robbed: Are you sure you want to take a life-and-death risk just to keep from losing some replaceable property?

The Southland Corporation, which operates the more than 5,000 "7-11" stores, has *ordered* its managers and employees not to try and defend themselves against a handgun robbery attempt. The Employee's Workbook, in its Violence Prevention Procedures section, says pointedly, "DON'T USE WEAPONS. *Southland policy forbids guns or other weapons in stores.* Weapons breed violence; it's dangerous to even have them in the store. The robber's weapon is already one too many."

Here are three recent newspaper headlines that tell of people who saw their attempts at self-defense backfire. They illustrate the great risk of death any time a handgun is drawn.

WOULD-BE HERO IS SLAIN, TWO WOUNDED IN HOLDUP

12-YEAR-OLD BOY DIES FROM GUNSHOT WOUND. FEAR LED FATHER TO WEAPON: NEED FOR PROTECTION ENDS IN TRAGEDY

STORE OWNER SHOT DEAD BY OWN PISTOL IN HOLDUP .

In the first case, which happened in Baltimore, Maryland, an elderly man was about to enter a drugstore when he saw through the window that a holdup was in progress. The elderly man, who was carrying a pistol, then hid around the corner and waited for the bandits to come out of the store. Inside, eleven people were on the floor, three employees and eight customers.

When the two robbers came out, the elderly man stepped out from his hiding place and shot one of them in the stomach. The wounded robber then shot the man in the chest, at close range, and he and his partner fled.

Next, one of the customers came out of the store. The elderly man, thinking this was a third robber, shot the customer in the shoulder, and then collapsed on the pavement. The robber survived, the innocent customer was wounded, and the elderly man died.

The second headline came from the Pottstown (Pennsylvania) *Mercury.* The father of the boy had bought a .22 pistol because of constant obscene telephone calls and three break-ins in the preceding two weeks. According to the newspaper:

> Sunday evening he was practicing with the gun on his property. He removed the ammunition clip and laid the gun down. His son, David, picked it up and was playing with it.
> "I never heard the shot," he recalled. "I just saw him fall. Police said there was one bullet left in the clip of the gun . . . All I can say to anyone who has a handgun in the house, get rid of it. It's not worth it . . . With children you just can't take the chance. People respect rifles, but not handguns."

The third headline, which appeared on March 12, 1981, in the Bridgeport (Connecticut) *Post,* concerned a liquor store owner who was killed by a robber who walked in and reached behind the counter for the owner's gun. The robber then shot the owner, apparently panicked, and ran out without taking any money. He did, however, take the handgun. The owner died.

The last sentence of the news account reads: "This was the seventh murder in the city this year . . ." Only two and a half months of the year had passed, yet this city of 148,000 had already seen seven of its citizens murdered.

Here is one more story, this from The *Kansas City Times,* April 20, 1981:

> GUN HANDLED BY FATHER GOES OFF, FATALLY WOUNDING DAUGHTER IN HEAD
> As relatives sitting down to Easter dinner looked on Sunday, a former gunsmith accidentally shot his only daughter in the head while showing her how to protect herself with a revolver.

The American Handgun War goes on, and on, and on . . .

HUNTING AND TARGET-SHOOTING

In my opinion, there is only one legitimate handgun sport and that is target-shooting. It is practiced at target ranges which are properly supervised and usually quite safe. Only certain handguns are true "sporting weapons," recognized as such by the sport's adherents.

On the other hand, "plinking"—shooting at tin cans and other small targets—in one's backyard is not and should not be considered a serious sport. When uncontrolled and unsupervised, it can be a very dangerous practice.

Some opponents of handgun control have claimed that we are out to stop all hunting and that controlling the handgun would severely affect hunting. That is simply untrue. Handgun control would in no way abridge the freedom of the true hunter. Few if any knowledgeable hunters consider the handgun an effective hunting weapon.

There *are* a few hunters who do hunt with handguns, but most states place restrictions on the type of guns that can be used in hunting, the reason being that killing of game should be done in as humane a manner as possible. Small-caliber handguns are more likely to wound the animal rather than kill it outright. Realistically, only long guns, rifles and shotguns are effective firearms for hunting.

People must understand that handguns and hunters are distinctly separate issues. Because the vast majority of hunters use a rifle or a shotgun, there is no reason why their pursuit of game (and sport) should be affected by handgun control. Mixing anti-hunting sentiment with the handgun issue confuses the killing of animals with the killing of people.

Two further reasons have been advanced to show why people should be allowed to own or acquire handguns without restriction. The first of the two, the Second Amendment argument which the NRA has worked so hard and spent so much time and money to implant in our minds, is that there is a constitutional right to own any type of firearm. Actually, I consider their argument an excuse, rather than a reason. The other "reason," the "macho" image argument, is more properly an explanation of an attitude or point of view which sheds some light on why certain types of people own, acquire, and use handguns.

THE SECOND AMENDMENT ARGUMENT

To understand the supposed constitutional argument it is essential that the reader be familiar with the *full and complete* wording of the Second Amendment to the Constitution of the United States. It reads: "A well-regulated Militia, being necessary to the security of a free State, the right of the people to keep and bear Arms, shall not be infringed." It would be interesting to take a poll of Americans and see how many have forgotten, or never knew, the Amendment's initial twelve words. Certainly, the pro-pistol lobby has not seen fit to clarify that point. The "militia" of the Amendment is what we all know today as the National Guard.

On five separate occasions, the Supreme Court of the United States has ruled that the Second Amendment was intended to protect members of a state militia from being disarmed by the federal government. In addition to those five Supreme Court decisions, the American Bar Association stated, in 1975, at its annual convention, that "every federal court decision involving the amendment has given the amendment a collective, militia interpretation and/or held that firearms-control laws enacted under a state's police power are constitutional."

The five cases in which the U.S. Supreme Court has ruled on the Second Amendment are: *U.S. v. Cruickshank* (1875); *Presser v. Illinois* (1886); *Miller v. Texas* (1894); *U.S. v. Miller* (1939); and *U.S. v. Tot* (1942).

In the mid-1970's, the NRA itself issued a pamphlet which contained an unusual—for the NRA—question and answer on this subject. It read:

Is there a constitutional safeguard for firearms owners? The Second Amendment to the United States Constitution says: "A well-regulated militia, being necessary to the security of a free State, the right of the people to keep and bear arms, shall not be infringed." While the NRA takes the firm stand that law-abiding Americans are constitutionally entitled to the legal ownership and use of firearms, the Second Amendment has not prevented firearms regulation on national and state levels. Also, the few federal court decisions involving the Second Amendment have largely given the Amendment a collective, militia interpretation and have limited the application of the Amendment to the federal government.

The constitutions of 37 states also contain a guarantee of the right to keep and bear arms. Nevertheless, the courts have repeatedly held that firearms-control laws enacted under a state's "police power" are constitutional.

Because of judicial precedent, then, the constitutional argument is of limited practical utility.

It should come as no surprise to anyone familiar with the current public stance of the NRA that this particular pamphlet is no longer available.

In fact, if we follow the NRA's current constitutional argument to its logical conclusion, then we could say that any American has a constitutional right to own *any* type of weapon—a bazooka, a tank, even a warplane!

THE "MACHO" IMAGE ARGUMENT

To many handgun buyers, owning a gun is a carry-over from the days of the Wild West, the frontier days, when the six-shooter made might, and might made the man. And in that era, one of the mightiest or most macho of men was Wyatt Earp—at least that is what many of today's handgun owners believe. Yet few of these present-day tough guys know that Earp was in fact an early proponent of handgun control. He went so far as to *ban* them inside city limits. There was a law in Dodge City that no one but law-enforcement officers was allowed to carry a six-shooter in public. Earp arrested anyone who broke this law.

Psychiatrists tell us that the great frontier still lives in the minds of men who buy handguns believing the weapon will give them a stronger sense of masculinity. The deadly nature of a handgun can make the smallest man bigger than the biggest *unarmed* man.

As we have seen time and time again, a loaded handgun in the possession of someone driven by emotion is a time bomb ready to explode. Examples are provided by almost any newspaper on almost any day.

Clarksville, Tennessee: "RUSSIAN ROULETTE GAME PROVES FATAL"

Austin, Texas: "FRIENDS TRIED TO STOP HIM, HE TRIED RUSSIAN ROULETTE—AND HE LOST"

Chicago, Illinois: "CHICAGO BOY, 9, DIES IN CLUB'S 'RUSSIAN
   ROULETTE' INITIATION
Indianapolis, Indiana: "DRIVER SHOT TO DEATH ON FREEWAY
   FOLLOWING RIGHT-OF-WAY DISPUTE"

What is far worse is the feeling of artificial superiority engen-
dered by the handgun which can and does breed violence. As
pointed out in a recent issue of *Psychology Today,* by University
of Wisconsin psychologist Leonard Berkowitz, "The mere sight of
a weapon can be a conditioned stimulus that evokes ideas and
motor responses associated with aggression." In simpler English:
while it is true that the finger pulls the trigger, the trigger may also
be pulling the finger—which certainly belies what the NRA says
in its favorite slogan: "Guns don't kill, people do."

When asked by a psychologist why they had used or obtained
handguns, inmates of a Florida prison told him that the main
reason was for "protection," and that if the felony they were about
to commit carried a prison term of ten to twenty years, they didn't
worry about the extra three years they might get because they had
used a handgun. Another common answer was that they had obtained a handgun because they would rather take the chance of
getting caught by the police for carrying an illegal weapon than
have their *friends* and *associates* find them without one. Apparently, it is not macho to be unarmed.

It would be nice to report that the prevalence of the macho
attitude is diminishing, but two personal experiences say that it is
not.

During a recent radio debate with one of the pro-pistol adherents, my opponent mentioned that he had been held up at knife-
point in the District of Columbia, but that it wouldn't have happened if he had been armed. He maintained that "This is an
instance where by obeying a gun law, a handgun law, I became
a victim of a crime." I guess he thought he could have whirled and
dropped his attacker with his "fast draw." In fact, I came away
with the distinct impression that he would have welcomed the
opportunity to try—to prove his manhood. Which of course ig-
nores the reality of the odds being against his succeeding.

The other anecdote is intensely personal. It involves something
that happened to me only a few weeks after my son Nick was shot

and killed in San Francisco. It was a Friday afternoon in Wilmington, and I'd left work early so I could stop on the way home and pick up a sportcoat I had bought.

On leaving the shopping center where the clothing store was located, I was about to pull into the two-lane street when I noticed a car coming up at a high rate of speed on the *shoulder* of the road, passing a string of cars that were stopped for a light.

The light was with me, so I pulled out, which meant the speeder had to slow down. He did so, but he began to blow his horn. Riled, I pulled into the center of the road, effectively taking up both lanes, and drove along at twenty-five miles an hour, half the speed the driver behind me had been doing when I first noticed him.

My tactic did more than just annoy him. He continued to blow his horn and to make rude gestures.

I had only two blocks to go before reaching the street where I would turn left, and when I got there I pulled over, leaving the right lane completely free. But instead of flashing past, my antagonist pulled up alongside me.

I turned to look at him, and saw to my horror that he was reaching into his glove compartment.

Suddenly, all of the details of his face blurred, and all I could see was the handgun that he was pointing at me out of the window.

He screamed, "Get your _____ ass over or I'll blow your _____ head off!"

I got over. And he roared off down the road.

Scared, startled, and shook up as I was, I tried to see his license plate number. Then I pulled off the road to let my heartbeat return to something like normal.

I knew I couldn't go home and tell Jeanne that she'd almost lost her husband too. The shock would be too much. So I drove to a friend's house and called the police. There was an investigation, but we just didn't have enough facts to go on. Whoever pointed that handgun at me is probably still out there somewhere, in my town. Knowing that is not a nice feeling.

So Mr. Macho scored one victory for the other side in the American Handgun War.

I would like to underline a point about the extent of violence in America today. It concerns the effect that all of these crimes have on us—whether we realize it or not.

It is said, and certainly my own experience bears it out, that until the violence touches you, no matter how great your concern may be, it still remains *concern* and not *action.*

We all deplore the statistics, and we shudder as we read the latest horror story in the newspaper or see the interview with the grieving survivors, but until we are touched personally we seldom take action.

But the point is we already *are* personally touched by the amount of violence in this country.

If you love to walk in the evening but aren't doing so because your neighborhood isn't "as safe as it once was," or you avoid seeing certain old friends because of where they live, or if you find yourself getting up in the middle of the night to double-check doors and windows, then you are already a casualty, already a victim of the American Handgun War.

4
WORLD OPINION, WORLD LAW

From the *Washington Post,* May 30, 1981:

SWISS TOURIST IS FATALLY SHOT
DURING ROBBERY IN SOUTHWEST

A Swiss woman who spoke no English was shot and killed in
Southwest Washington Saturday night by a man who robbed her and
two other members of her tour group as they took an after-dinner
stroll near their hotel.

Police speculated that the victim, Mrs. T. Eggimann, about 60, may
have been shot because neither she nor the two women with her
could understand the robber who took their handbags . . .

Robbi Williman, the tour leader, said he had advised the group to
avoid the side streets near the hotel at night.

"I told them not to go on the side streets," he said.

It is sad that the differences between this visitor's homeland and
her chosen vacation spot turned out to be so great.

Of all the Western European democracies, Switzerland appears
to be closest to the United States in its attitude toward private gun
ownership. But, as is so often the case, appearances are misleading.
The reason the Swiss keep guns at home is quite different. And so
is the result.

According to the information Handgun Control, Inc. obtained
from the Swiss Embassy, here are some facts about gun ownership
and gun control in Switzerland:

All male Swiss citizens incorporated in combat militia units are taught how to shoot, beginning at age twenty with basic military training . . .

The military authorities keep an exact record of all military rifles and pistols kept in the homes of Swiss militia members . . .

Commercial sales of handguns are only allowed to persons presenting a duly signed "firearms purchase certificate" issued by the competent authorities of the canton (state) where the purchaser is domiciled . . .

Such purchase certificates are not issued to persons under eighteen years of age, to mentally ill or deficient people, to persons under interdiction, to habitual drinkers under protective guardianship, to different categories of persons with a criminal record as well as persons where there is reason to assume that, in using a weapon, they might present a danger to themselves or others . . .

Persons authorized to sell handguns . . . are required to keep detailed records containing the date of sale, the exact personal data of the purchaser, the number, issuing authority and date of the "purchase certificate" as well as the type and factory number of the firearm . . .

Or, as the *New York Times* put it (in a 1978 article):

Most Swiss have a gun at home, but the country has one of the lowest crime rates in the world.

Ownership of weapons is widespread because all Swiss men have to undergo annual military training and must take the army rifle and ammunition home after the training course. They are the only soldiers in the world to do so.

According to federal statistics, Swiss courts handled only 31 homicide cases in 1974 and 33 in 1975. Other crimes involving use of firearms in this nation of six million people are also few.

Moreover, officials say that the army weapons are not a significant factor in what crime there is.

"In cases of crimes, murderers will not generally use the army rifle . . . it's not as handy as a pistol."

One of the most startling differences between Mrs. Eggimann's native land and the United States is that in 1978, a year in which we had over 9,582 handgun deaths, Switzerland had only *34*. As a result of statistics like these, some foreign journalists tell me they would much rather be *war* correspondents than be assigned to Washington, D.C., and have to walk its streets at night.

The rest of the civilized world looks with horror at the lack of gun controls in the United States. Here is a cross-section of world press reaction to the near-killing of President Reagan:

The Financial Times of London: "This twist of fate, of such significance to so many countries, must surely clinch the case against the laxity of [U.S.] gun laws."

Le Monde, Paris: "How many of these assassination attempts that traumatize a whole society would be avoided if people like John Hinckley, Jr. couldn't buy revolvers?"

Frankfurter Rundschau, Frankfurt: "Perhaps President Reagan will now change his position on gun control."

Corriere della Sera, Milan: "A secret, violent part of America explodes every once in a while like the hidden vein of a volcano."

Svenska Dagbladet, Stockholm: "Since Kennedy was assassinated . . . violence in the U.S. has increased alarmingly . . . but Americans have not been able to . . . make it more difficult to get weapons."

De Telegraaf, Amsterdam: "As long as nothing is done [about gun control] the possibility remains that the career of any President can be cut short by a bullet."

The Gazette, Montreal: "It is ironic that an opponent of gun control . . . should now have attracted a gunman's anger, envy, or twisted desire for notoriety."

Winnipeg Free Press, Canada: "Rigorous gun control . . . would have made [the shooting] less likely to happen. Making tragedy less likely is the duty of responsible lawmakers."

Jerusalem Post, Israel: "The reckless abandon with which [Americans] treat the lives of their leaders is a threat . . . to the world."

Daily Nation, Nairobi, Kenya: "Guns are all too easily available in today's American society."

Straits Times, Singapore: "The U.S. has preserved for its people the liberty to kill almost at will."

Asahi Shimbun, Tokyo: "We fear that superior talent will stop seeking political careers, and that, above all, other countries will lose confidence in America."

The Age, Melbourne, Australia: "Americans have become their own worst enemies."

It all comes down to this: the United States is the only major country in the world without effective national handgun controls.

By way of comparison:

In England, according to Rudolf Klein, a professor of social policy studies at the University of Bath:

> British law is predicated on the simple principle that possession of a weapon is a privilege rather than a right. Licenses are granted by the police, who register all guns. It is up to applicants to justify their motives for ownership rather than an obligation of the authorities to explain their reasons for refusal.
>
> Applicants for a weapon of any kind must first fill in a three-page form, which requires among other things the guarantee that the gun will be stored out of reach of burglars.
>
> The applicant must also prove that he has never been convicted of a criminal offense or suffered from mental disorder. He can be denied a license as well if he has a record of alcoholism or even heavy drinking.
>
> Next, the applicant is interviewed by a police officer, who is likely to conduct an investigation among the potential gun-owner's neighbors and friends in order to collect information on his background. Any "character defect" is cause for rejection of a license.
>
> Finally, the applicant must persuade the police that his possession of a weapon is necessary—and [that] is the hard part of the exercise.
>
> Gun collectors and members of approved rifle clubs are generally given approval, on condition that their weapons are kept in secure places. But self-defense and the protection of property are not regarded as adequate reasons for permits.

In April 1981, as reported by the *Los Angeles Daily Journal:*

> One of Britain's chief law-enforcement officers, speaking in Los Angeles this week, touted strict gun controls as one of the leading factors which keeps violent crimes committed with firearms to a relatively low level in the United Kingdom. James T. Jardine, national chairman of the Police Federation of England and Wales, stated that while murder in the U.K. has increased 50 percent in the last ten years [during which period it *doubled* in the U.S.],

statistics show that only one out of six are committed with a gun [U.S.: seven out of ten]. Jardine . . . explained that laws in Britain make it extremely difficult to secure a license for a handgun . . . Prime Minister Thatcher, he noted, has only had an egg thrown at her.

It is hard to disagree with Professor Klein's comment that: "We cannot help but believe that Americans ought to share the basic premise of our gun legislation—that the availability of firearms breeds violence."

In Canada, there have been far tougher handgun-control laws for years.

According to University of Toronto law professor Martin L. Friedland, writing only a week after the attempt on President Reagan's life:

We have never had to face a situation as in the United States today, which appears to many observers to be almost out of control. The Canadian system combines limitations on the reasons for possession of handguns, careful screening of applicants, vigorous judicial sentencing, and strong federal action. It may be that the United States has something to learn from Canada on this issue.

In 1979 there were fewer than 60 homicides committed with handguns in all of Canada. Metropolitan Toronto, with more than two million people, had only four handgun homicides last year. In contrast, in 1979 handguns were used in almost 900 killings in New York City, about 300 in metropolitan Detroit, and 75 in metropolitan Boston. The handgun homicide rate in Canada hovers around 10 percent of all homicides. In the United States it is about 50 percent.

For almost 100 years, Canada has controlled the possession of handguns. The total number of registered handguns in Canada at the end of 1979 (including handguns owned by the police) was approximately 750,000 weapons. In contrast, there were 2 million new handguns sold in the United States in 1980. One quarter of all U.S. households have at least one handgun.

In Canada, a person can acquire a handgun in connection with his lawful occupation (police officer or security guard) or for target practice if a member of an approved club. Collectors can acquire handguns, but since 1979 the law which then read that a person could acquire a handgun to protect "life or property" now reads only "to protect life." In 1979, Canadian authorities issued only 5,000 such licenses, and that number included police handguns.

In Japan, according to Japanese journalist Yasushi Hara, hand-gun-control laws are perhaps the strictest in the world:

> We Japanese frankly find it difficult to understand how Americans can tolerate the existence of some 90 million guns in the United States. For our own laws are such that the possession of firearms by private individuals is so restricted that crimes involving guns are a rarity.
>
> The paradox in this is that our extraordinarily strict gun controls were laid down by the U.S. military establishment that governed Japan after World War II. The occupation authorities, headed by General Douglas MacArthur, decreed that the possession of firearms was the gravest of offenses.
>
> . . . Under Japanese law, the only persons allowed to carry handguns are government security officials. The sole exception to this rule are athletes undergoing pistol training in order to compete in shooting events . . .
>
> It strikes me as clear that there is a distinct correlation between gun control laws and the rate of violent crime. The fewer the guns, the less the violence. We are largely indebted to the United States for this fortunate situation. But we cannot quite comprehend that Americans cannot do for themselves what they did for us.

In Mexico, there is a problem created not by Mexicans but by gun smugglers *from the United States.* In testimony before a Senate subcommittee in 1978, a Treasury Department official said, "Traffic in firearms to Mexico is a serious problem and de-serves attention, particularly since part of the problem stems from the comparatively easy accessibility of firearms in the United States."

More recently, another Treasury Department official told the Associated Press that "most guns smuggled out of the United States were destined for Mexico." He said that the black market flourishes because of the strict Mexican handgun law.

It is possible to get a license to own and carry a handgun in

Mexico, but the requirements are stiff. One of them, interestingly, requires that the applicant already have fulfilled his obligation to the national military service.

Doesn't it strike you as rather strange that both of our neighbors —Canada and Mexico—have far more stringent handgun laws than we do?

The firearms-control laws in Italy, France, Israel, and West Germany are equally strict. The shooting of Pope John Paul II might lead people to think that Italy has relatively loose handgun laws. But it does not. In fact, the gun used to shoot the leader of the Catholic faith was smuggled into the country by a foreign terrorist.

Italian gun laws have become consistently and progressively more stringent since 1930. A 1975 law calls for police clearance in order to acquire or transfer arms, and requires that the grounds for acquisition or transfer be specified; the law also limits the number of guns an individual who is not a collector may own (two handguns and six hunting or sporting rifles or shotguns per person) and requires a license if one wants to carry a handgun outside the home.

In France, elaborate background checks are carried out on any French citizen who wants to own a handgun. He or she must be eighteen, have permission from a "person exercising parental authority," and loss of the weapon must be reported to the police promptly. According to the French Embassy in Washington, "Requests for authorization must be accompanied by the appropriate documents; permits will only be issued after it has been verified that the individual has no criminal record. The authorization to purchase a weapon is valid for three months from the date of issue; beyond that time it becomes null and void unless an extension is granted. Permits to acquire and own weapons and ammunition may be rescinded for reasons having to do with public order and individual security by the authority that granted them initially . . . The penalties are very severe for any person convicted of carrying a weapon for which he has no permit. Prison sentences of up to ten years may be imposed . . ."

In Israel, as David Shipler of the *New York Times* wrote after the Reagan shooting, the country "is pervaded by guns but not excited by them . . . 'America and Israel are both immigrant societies,' said a political scientist at Hebrew University, 'but immigrants to America come as individuals, whereas in Israel people immigrate as part of a people, and therefore the conceptions of security are different.' " He went on to say that Israelis view the gun as related to collective security and not, as do Americans, individual protection. "When we see individuals carrying guns, we see them almost as organs of the community."

Anyone caught armed without a permit in Israel can get as many as seven years in prison, and the sale of ammunition is strictly regulated. No one under twenty or on active military duty can get a private permit, and instruction is mandatory. There are just over 150,000 licensed handguns in Israel.

In West Germany a buyer must prove a specific need. Not only must he prove training or experience but he must also take an exam in the presence of a police officer and a licensed civilian. There are different types of licenses and permits in West Germany, some of which allow the gun owner to keep the weapon only at his residence or place of business and not to carry it outside (which requires a separate "license to carry"). Criteria for ownership are tough.

The gun problem in our country as compared to other countries has been described graphically by many writers. Below are quotations from two articles which are not particularly recent, but which describe situations that, unfortunately, remain today.

The first is from a 1974 article in the *Wall Street Journal* by one of the country's most respected gun control experts, Franklin E. Zimring of the University of Chicago, who served as director of research for the Eisenhower Commission's staff report on "Firearms and Violence in American Life."

A TALE OF TWO CITIES

If you have a Detroit friend seeking a relatively safe vacation in a setting of near-civil war, the place for him to go is Belfast, Northern Ireland.

Not that it's dull in Northern Ireland. Since 1960 the rate of death from violence has increased more than twentyfold. In the peak year of 1972, a total of 476 persons were slain: 76 percent of the casualties were civilians. Since January 1969 more than 1,000 people were bombed or shot to death in that small country—a reign of terror sufficient to draw world attention to "bloody Ulster," and to require British military occupation and preventive detention.

But as the latest FBI reports show, your Detroit friend will be relatively safe in Northern Ireland—about four times as safe as at home. It happens that the city of Detroit (1,513,000) has almost exactly the same population as the whole of Northern Ireland (1,536,000). Yet in 1973 alone, Detroit police reported 751 deaths from criminal homicide, 24 more than the total number of civilians killed in Ulster during the five and a half years from the beginning of the "troubles" in 1969 through the end of this past June.

Of course, there are safer places to live than in Northern Ireland but surprisingly few of them are major American cities. During the past decade, violent killing in American cities has more than doubled. In 1973 each of the ten largest American cities had a homicide rate higher than that of Northern Ireland.

The second quotation is from an article written by *Washington Post* reporter Don Oberdorfer on April 20, 1975, under the heading, "The World's Largest City Is Also the Safest."

According to official data, Tokyo, with 11.6 million people, had 189 murders last year. This compares to 1,554 murders in New York, with 7.9 million people and 277 in Washington, a city of 723,000. Tokyo reported 425 robberies last year, compared to 77,940 in New York, and 7,941 in Washington. Tokyo reported 420 rapes (New York, 4,054; Washington, 2,911).

Oberdorfer explains that while some of the reasons for the startling differences in the figures relating to violence in the two countries are cultural, credit must also be given to the fact that, as mentioned earlier, handguns are forbidden to Japanese citizens.

Not a single person was killed by a handgun in Tokyo last year, and police reported only ten incidents in which handguns were involved . . . Due to the relative scarcity of weapons, most of the gun battles in Japan are strictly limited to television and motion-picture dramas. According to Metropolitan Police records—Tokyo police fired their service revolvers in action only four times in all of 1974. Two of those were warning shots in the air.

All of this is not to say that a law which works in Japan, Sweden, England, or even nearby Canada can be transplanted to America. But the evidence is overwhelming. The facts identify our lack of effective handgun laws as our all-too-fatal flaw—as Mrs. Eggimann, the Swiss tourist, found out in our nation's capital.

Our ad (and poster) below says it all.

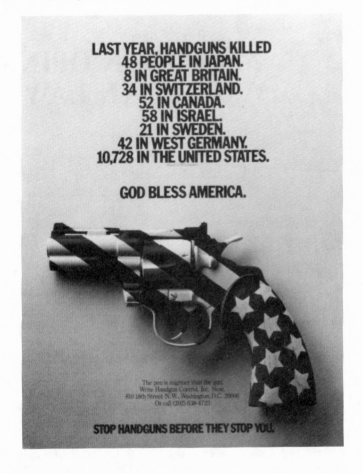

**LAST YEAR, HANDGUNS KILLED
48 PEOPLE IN JAPAN.
8 IN GREAT BRITAIN.
34 IN SWITZERLAND.
52 IN CANADA.
58 IN ISRAEL.
21 IN SWEDEN.
42 IN WEST GERMANY.
10,728 IN THE UNITED STATES.**

GOD BLESS AMERICA.

The pen is mightier than the gun.
Write Handgun Control, Inc. Now.
810 18th Street N.W., Washington, D.C. 20006
Or call (202) 638-4723

STOP HANDGUNS BEFORE THEY STOP YOU.

5
AMERICAN OPINION, AMERICAN LAW

RIGHT after Nick's murder I would have given anything to be able to live in a society that had no handguns at all. Or, better yet, a society that felt no *need* to own handguns.

And I said so, which echoed the early position of Handgun Control, Inc., then still known as the National Council to Control Handguns. Their first board of directors had endorsed a federal bill which called for banning the manufacture, sale, and possession of handguns (except for the law-enforcement community, security guards, and target-shooters whose handguns would be kept at secure ranges).

Yet I was uncomfortable with this position, especially as I learned more and more about the level of crime and violence in our society and the resultant fear, about how other countries dealt with the problem, and about how the American people felt about the various forms of handgun control.

All of this led me, gradually, away from NCCH's initial position and toward the provisions contained in today's bill supported by Handgun Control, Inc. But that came later.

One thing was clear to me from the start. In America, resort to the handgun had become commonplace.

Headlines alone tell the grisly stories:

ARGUMENT OVER REFRIGERATOR ENDS IN OMAHAN'S DEATH

MAN KILLED IN DISPUTE OVER PARKING SPACE

EMPLOYEE REFUSES LUNCH, KILLED

QUARREL OVER DOG LEADS TO DEATH

CURSING OFFENDED BAR PATRON, AND 2 MEN DIED

WOMAN DIES ON WEDDING DAY

In every one of these cases, the instrument of death was a small, easily concealable handgun. Is it any wonder that most Americans want national handgun control?

PUBLIC OPINION

For almost half a century, public opinion pollsters have been asking Americans if they want controls on handguns, and Americans have been saying yes, yes, yes.

What, exactly, have these polls reported? Well, in 1938, when George Gallup first asked, "Do you think all owners of pistols and revolvers should be required to register with the government?," the answer was 79 percent "yes," and only 15 percent "no."

Since then, public opinion polls have continued to show that the majority of Americans want *some* form of *national* gun control. As the focus of proposed legislation has narrowed from "all firearms" to "handguns," these polls have become more specialized, surveying the public's reaction to specific legislative proposals ranging from registration and permissive licensing to severe restrictions on the sale and possession of handguns.

The most recent Gallup Poll indicated that *91 percent of the American people favored some form of handgun control.* Perhaps more striking is the fact that the majority of gun owners back some form of handgun control.

In examining these polls, it is important to recognize that, until now, with the growth of Handgun Control, Inc., there has *never* been a national education or national lobbying campaign to promote a specific approach to the handgun problem. Even so, significant support has existed for even the most severe measures.

The most recent opportunity for voters to decide on a clearly drawn handgun-control issue occurred in the state of Massachusetts during the 1976 elections. *People vs. Handguns,* a citizens group, gathered 102,000 certified signatures in order to place on the ballot a referendum proposing the most extreme form of handgun control: a prohibition on all civilian possession of handguns. The referendum was defeated by 70 to 30 percent.

Immediately, the pro-gun lobby hailed the vote as a repudiation of all handgun control measures. However, a more accurate picture of the vote was obtained when Cambridge Survey Research, Inc. did a post-election survey of Massachusetts voters and found that the main reason for the defeat was economic.

Seventy percent of the voters felt that the proposed handgun ban would be too expensive—because the state would be obligated to buy back all handguns from citizens. Sixty-three percent of the voters polled mentioned taxes and unemployment as the most important problem facing the state. The handgun proposal was among eight other items voted down; all of them involved additional cost to the taxpayers.

The pollsters then questioned the Massachusetts voters on other forms of handgun control, and got the following results:

90 percent of the voters favored a waiting period prior to a handgun purchase to check the criminal record of the purchaser of the handgun.

89 percent favored the licensing of handgun owners and the registration of handguns.

82 percent favored a ban on the sale of small, cheap Saturday Night Specials.

67 percent of the voters agreed that the only way to ban handguns is by federal law, since state laws which allow handguns to be purchased in some states and not others are ineffective.

54 percent favored limiting the number of handguns manufactured.

54 percent favored a ban on concealable handguns.

Only 3 percent of the voters said there should be no controls on guns.

Clearly, the referendum in Massachusetts was defeated because of adverse economic factors—and *not* the attitude of the citizenry about the merits of handgun control.

But what about the feeling in the rest of the country? In 1978, the Center for the Study and Prevention of Handgun Violence commissioned a *national* survey of public attitudes toward handgun controls. Because of their experience with the 1976 Massachusetts survey, the Center chose Cambridge Reports (a division of Cambridge Surveys) to do the research. This survey was the first truly in-depth national poll on handgun attitudes.

According to Cambridge Reports, "The survey was conducted to measure citizen awareness of, knowledge, of, and attitude toward handguns and control of handguns in this country. The survey is based on 1,500 personal interviews conducted with a sample that was selected to reflect the views of the adult population of the United States."

A brief summary of their findings makes the following observations:

Handguns are extremely common in the United States. One household in four has a handgun in it. Almost half of the time, the handgun was purchased in order to provide protection, although only 3 percent of the population has actually used a handgun in self-defense.

4 percent of the public has had an accident with a handgun; the incidence of such accidents is almost as high among those who do not have a handgun in their homes as among those who do.

One American adult in nine has survived an attack with a handgun.

One respondent in five reports a close friend has been attacked or threatened with a handgun; one in eight says a member of the family has been attacked or threatened with a handgun.

Roughly one person in four thinks he or she will quite likely experience handgun violence firsthand sometime during their lifetime.

On the question of policy, the report states:

It is clear that the vast majority of the public (both those who live with handguns and those who do not) want handgun licensing and registration.

More than three respondents in four say that people should be required to obtain a permit to purchase a handgun and that owners should register their handguns at the time of purchase and participate in a registration program for handguns currently in circulation.

More than 75 percent of the public wants license regulations for carrying handguns outside the home.

The survey also found, as I had suspected it would, that "only one-third of the country goes as far as to call for buying back and destroying all existing handguns. A similar number favor banning all private ownership of handguns. Clearly a majority of the public is not interested in carrying handgun control measurses to those lengths. *But they do support fundamental controls on handguns."* (My italics.)

The pollsters observed: "When it comes to handgun controls, people are quite prepared to put their votes where their principles are. When asked whether they would be more inclined or less inclined to vote for a candidate who favors handgun controls, we find that seven respondents would be more inclined to vote for the handgun-control candidate for every four who would be less inclined."

Regarding the pro-pistol lobby's charge that those who favor handgun controls are "soft on criminals," the report points out: "The public not only wants to keep track of who has guns and where they are and how they are used, but also, Americans come down hard on people who have misused guns. Eighty-three percent of the public wants mandatory prison sentences for all persons using a gun in a crime." That happens also to be my position, and that of Handgun Control, Inc.

The summary concludes:

Because present regulations governing the purchase and use of handguns vary so much from one state to another and make control of handguns difficult, if not impossible, 70 percent of all U.S. voters want to see handgun control mandated nationally and look to the federal government for that legislation.

In short, while a sizeable portion of the people in this country own handguns, both people who own handguns and those who do not want some assurance that small guns will only be in the hands of responsible people and that accountability through licensing will exist. It is clear from the overwhelming favorable response to proposed regulations governing the purchase, use, and licensing of handguns that the American public wants some form of handgun-control legislation.

We have all heard and read a great deal in the last year about the American public becoming more conservative. If true, increasing conservatism does not affect the public's desire for handgun controls, as two very recent polls have pointed out.

In the spring of 1981, George Gallup reported that an amazingly high percentage 81 percent—of the public are in favor of requiring a license for anyone who wants to carry a handgun outside the home. Gallup said, "Public support for tough gun legislation has increased sharply since a year ago, with 62 percent of the Americans now favoring adoption of a law similar to Massachusetts' Bartley-Fox statute in their own states."

The Bartley-Fox law, passed in 1975, requires people to have a license to carry a pistol outside the home, and a mandatory sentence of one year in jail for anyone convicted of carrying a gun without a license.

Gallup also reconfirmed the public's attitude about a total ban: "Although support has grown for tough gun laws, and while a large majority continues to favor stricter laws covering the sale of pistols, the public continued to vote against an outright ban . . . One possible explanation for the apparent inconsistency between support for stricter gun laws and opposition to a ban on pistols is that the growing fear of crime has caused many people to believe that they need a gun for protection—a false security measure in the opinion of many experts."

Results of another recent poll appeared in *Time* magazine's June 1, 1981 issue. The *Time* poll confirmed a large conservative swing in the country, but *Time* saw the public's attitude toward gun control as an exception.

When asked whether or not they favored *mandatory* registration of handguns, 60 percent of the respondents said "yes," as opposed to 37 percent who said "no." *Time* called it "a stand that once again disagrees with the position of the New Right."

To some readers, 60 percent may not seem like an especially

impressive majority, but it should be understood that the pro-pistol lobby has consistently argued that mandatory registration is one of the most stringent steps the government could take in this area because, claims the NRA, it would lead to the ulti-mate disarming of the American people by an autocratic federal government. And yet, 60 percent of the American people *at a time when the very idea of government control is highly un-popular* are saying they favor mandatory registration of hand-guns.

The significance of this cannot be overstressed. At a time when Americans are saying no to so many other types of government regulation, a time when one of the hottest words in Washington is *"de*regulation," the *people* are saying that the government should—no, *must*—regulate handguns. To my way of thinking, that is a very important and hopeful sign.

AMERICAN LAWS—FEDERAL

An excellent short history of efforts toward firearms control on the federal level, in the House Judiciary Committee Report of May 6, 1976, notes that "A bill banning interstate commerce in handguns was first introduced in both houses in 1915. Con-gress first exercised its constitutional power of taxation in the fire-arms field by levying a 10 percent manufacturer's excise tax on those commodities in 1919." The report observed that there were "expressions of concern over handguns as a potential public safety problem" even then, more than sixty years earlier. In 1924, "No fewer than a dozen bills seeking to restrict the flow of handguns interstate were introduced and in 1927 the receiving by private individuals of firearms capable of being concealed on the person through the United States mail was pro-hibited by law."

In 1934, the Department of Justice began to seek congressional support to broaden federal control over firearms. The result was the National Firearms Act of 1934 (NFA) which provided for fed-eral jurisdiction over intrastate as well as interstate transactions in such firearms as the Thompson submachine gun (the "tommy gun") along with "machine guns, sawed-off shotguns, silencers and other, less common types of ordnance." At the same time the Justice Department proposed federal handgun registration, but the proposal was deleted from the bill in the House of Representatives.

Four years later, according to the Judiciary Committee history, the Federal Firearms Act of 1938 (FFA) "sought to check the free flow of more common types of firearms by prohibiting certain classes of persons from possessing them, establishing a fee-supported licensing system for manufacturers, importers, and dealers [the fee schedule for licenses was $25, $25, and $1, respectively], and vesting enforcement authority in the Department of the Treasury, which was in turn delegated to the Internal Revenue Service." In the 1938 Act Congress for the first time set forth several categories of individuals who, by definition, were "unfit to possess firearms."

In 1957, soon after the importation of foreign-manufactured rifles and new and military surplus handguns began to be a problem, the Secretary of the Treasury called for "serialization of all firearms and changes in federal dealer record-keeping requirements, including the requirement that they be maintained permanently. Regulations finally adopted required dealers to maintain records for 10 years and .22-caliber rifles were exempted from the serialization requirements."

Following the assassination of President Kennedy in 1963 with a World War II foreign mail-order rifle, there was

> . . . renewed congressional interest in reducing firearms violence. Although a bill covering mail-order traffic in rifles and shotguns and one embodying President Johnson's request for increased firearms regulation died in committee in the 87th and 89th Congresses, a bill increasing licensing fees and strengthening federal regulation of dealers, establishing minimum-age requirements for handgun and long-gun purchases and prohibiting handgun sales to out-of-state residents was reported by the Senate Judiciary Committee . . . as part of the Omnibus Crime Control and Safe Streets Act of 1968 . . . The proposal passed both houses and was approved within weeks of the assassinations of Senator Robert F. Kennedy and Dr. Martin Luther King . . . On October 22, 1968, both houses approved H.R. 17735 (Gun Control Act of 1968).

The Judiciary Committee pointed out that "the handgun, as a primary implement in the commission of violent crimes and a potential threat to public safety, has been the consistent subject of public concern in the firearms area."

Since the Gun Control Act of 1968 Congress has continued to focus on the handgun as a key factor in the fight against crime and violence. The Judiciary Committee winds up its short history of federal gun control efforts as follows:

> In 1973, the Senate passed a bill which would have applied to domestically produced handguns the same minimum criteria that the Department of the Treasury uses to determine whether foreign handguns are fit for importation under the "sporting purposes" test of the Act. Although the bill was not reported by this Committee, it brought to the fore public attention to the cheap, easily concealable "Saturday Night Special," a term attached to the type of handgun most often purchased in Detroit during the 1967 disturbances. In the 93rd Congress as well, more than 130 firearms-related bills were introduced, and they were as disparate and wide-ranging as those referred to the Subcommittee in this Congress. Then, as now, the overriding concern was the handgun.

Surprisingly, despite all of this detailed attention to the issue, soon after the 1968 Gun Control Act went into effect, it became quickly apparent the new law had many loopholes. Although the importation of "non-sporting" handguns was prohibited, the importation of their *parts* was not. Certain companies immediately began to import parts and assemble them domestically. As mentioned in Chapter 2, it was this kind of gun assembled from imported parts which was used to shoot President Reagan. Nor have any controls been placed on secondary transfers of handguns (private transactions between non-dealers). And although one is required to fill out a form and answer certain questions when purchasing a firearm from a dealer, there is no required verification procedure to ascertain the validity of the purchaser's identity, whether he or she has a criminal record, and whether other questions (such as any history of mental illness, drug dependency, etc.) have been answered truthfully.

AMERICAN LAWS—STATE AND LOCAL

The body count resulting from the American Handgun War would suggest that there are no effective or well-intentioned laws *anywhere* in the country. This is not true. Recognizing the ever-increasing spiral of handgun violence in their own regions, communities, cities, counties, and even states have passed tougher handgun restrictions. But too often their neighbors have non-existent or weak handgun laws, and thus the good laws are easily bypassed and, in effect, defeated.

A clear example is Washington, D.C., which in 1977 passed one of the strictest handgun control laws in the nation. Only the police and security guards may legally buy and carry handguns in the nation's capital. Edward D. Jones, III, a former Justice Department analyst, made a study comparing handgun homicides in 1974 with handgun homicides in 1978, the first full year of the law's existence. It showed that family killings decreased from 10 percent of all handgun homicides in 1974 to 5 percent in 1978, and that handgun-caused homicides among neighbors, lovers, and other "non-family" acquaintances dropped from 44 percent to 38 percent of the total.

However, the study also showed that the new law had little impact on the use of handguns in street crimes. The reason for this, according to Jones, is that the criminal can follow his "single-minded intention to engage in criminality" by the simple expedient of buying a handgun elsewhere. It is no trouble at all to drive across the bridge into Virginia and buy a handgun with hardly any questions asked; from some points in the District of Columbia, the drive is as short as ten minutes.

Other studies have shown that of all the handguns confiscated in crimes in the District of Columbia, almost a third came from Virginia. On the average, only 10 percent came from the District itself. To cite a prominent example, the handgun used to wound President Reagan was not acquired in Washington, D.C. It was purchased, easily, in a Dallas, Texas, pawnshop and easily transported across several states because it was no problem to conceal it.

The pro-handgun lobby likes to cite New York State's Sullivan Law as an example of a tough handgun law that does not work.

Some background may be helpful. In 1911, it was only a misdemeanor in New York to carry an unlicensed concealed weapon, and pawnshops lined Park Row, offering pistols at prices ranging from three to six dollars. According to a New York State document, youth gangs roamed the Lower East Side on the prowl for victims. In addition to the many robberies, there were also an alarming number of killings and maimings. Clearly, the situation was intolerable.

A committee of prominent citizens was formed—including Bernard Baruch's father Simon, Nathan Straus, John Wanamaker, and John D. Rockefeller, Jr. Timothy D. Sullivan, a prominent political leader, and the successor to "Boss" Tweed, effectively joined forces with this group which proposed sweeping changes in the penal law. In part because of Sullivan's impassioned speech on the Senate floor, a new law was passed which made it a felony, rather than a misdemeanor, to carry a concealed weapon without a license. Because of his efforts, the law carries his name.

Probably because the Sullivan law was extremely tough, especially as amended over the years, a Treasury Department study in the early 1970's (Project Identification) showed that over 90 percent of the handguns used in crime in New York came from out of the state. It was the same old picture: because there is no *federal* law, once a state passes a stringent handgun law, the handguns begin to flow in from states where there are weak laws. For example, the handgun used to kill John Lennon was acquired in Hawaii and that used to kill former Congressman Allard Lowenstein came from Connecticut.

In August 1980, in response to yet another wave of handgun violence in New York, the Sullivan law was strengthened significantly by adding a *mandatory* prison sentence for carrying an unlicensed handgun.

State and local laws affecting the availability of handguns are a patchwork of some 20,000 different ordinances, definitions, and requirements. Following is a summary list of all state handgun laws in the United States. It was prepared for Handgun Control, Inc. by Philip J. Cook, associate director of the Institute of Policy Science and Public Affairs at Duke University.

The following sampling of firearms laws from five states is also based on material prepared by Philip Cook of Duke University.

STATE HANDGUN REGULATIONS[1]

	Dealers License	*Police Check on Buyer*[2]	*Minimum Waiting Period (Days)*[3]	*Registration*[4]	*Carrying Concealed*[5]
New England					
Maine					L
New Hampshire	X			D	P
Vermont					
Massachusetts	X	PP,ID		D	L
Rhode Island	X	AP	3		L
Connecticut	X	AP	14	D	L
Middle Atlantic					
New York	X	PP		O	L
New Jersey	X	PP	7	D	L
Pennsylvania	X	AP	2	D	L
East North Central					
Ohio					P
Indiana	X	AP	7		L
Illinois		ID	3		P
Michigan		PP		D,O	L
Wisconsin			2		P
West North Central					
Minnesota		AP	7	D	L
Iowa	X	PP	3	D	L
Missouri		PP			P
North Dakota	X	PP		D	L
South Dakota	X	AP	2	D	L
Nebraska					P
Kansas					P
South Atlantic					
Delaware	X				L
Maryland	X	AP	7	D	L
District of Columbia	X	Ban on transfers		O	L
Virginia[6]					L
West Virginia					L
North Carolina	X	PP			P
South Carolina	X			D	L
Georgia	X				P
Florida					L

	Dealers License	Police Check on Buyer[2]	Minimum Waiting Period (Days)[3]	Registration[4]	Carrying Concealed[5]
East South Central					
Kentucky					P
Tennessee	X	AP	15		P
Alabama	X	AP	2	D	L
Mississippi				D,O	P
West South Central					
Arkansas					
Louisiana					P
Oklahoma					P
Texas	X				P
Mountain					
Montana					L
Idaho					L
Wyoming					L
Colorado					L
New Mexico					
Arizona					P
Utah				D	L
Nevada					L
Pacific					
Washington	X	AP	3	D	L
Oregon	X	AP	5	D	L
California	X	AP	15	D	L
Alaska					P
Hawaii	X	PP		O	L
Percentage of U.S. Population	59%	60%	42%	50%	98%

[1]Source: Edward D. Jones III and Marla Wilson Ray, *Handgun Control: Strategies, Enforcement, and Effectiveness* (Office for Improvements in the Administration of Justice, U.S. Department of Justice, March 1980).

[2]*Police Check on Buyer:* AP—An "Application to Purchase" a handgun must be filed with the relevant state or local authorities; the transfer can take place only if the application is not denied during the stipulated waiting period. Silence on the part of authorities implies consent.

ID—A firearm owner's identification card must be obtained from the state before taking possession of any firearm. This card must be renewed every few years.

PP—A "Permit to Purchase" must be obtained from the relevant state or local authorities before each handgun purchase.

[3]*Minimum Waiting Period:* Minimum time which must elapse between the purchase and the actual transfer of a handgun. This waiting period is usually imposed

in connection with an "AP" system, in order to give the authorities (usually the police) a chance to screen the application. (In most cases there is also some delay in the PP systems connected with a police check of the permit applicant's criminal record.) The length of the statutory waiting time gives some indication of how thoroughly the authorities check the applicant's record.

[4]*Registration:* D—Dealers must report the sale of each handgun to either state or local authorities, who in most states keep a permanent record. This reporting and record-keeping constitute "registration" because the reports include information on both the buyer and the gun. Sales by nondealers are also covered by this requirement in some states.

O—Handgun owners must register their guns with the authorities.

[5]*Carrying Concealed:* P—Prohibited, with certain exceptions (such as law-enforcement officers, military personnel, and certain security guards).

L—A special license is required to carry a concealed weapon. In some states, this license is also required to carry a handgun openly. It should be noted that the typical penalties for violation of this requirement differ widely among jurisdictions.

[6]Virginia imposes a PP system and handgun dealer licensing on counties with population density exceeding 1,000 per square mile.

ILLINOIS

This large midwestern state requires that anyone who wants to purchase a handgun must obtain what it calls a "Firearms Owner's Identification Card." A notorized application, plus a photo, is sent to the Illinois Department of Law Enforcement. This agency then runs a computer check for criminal record (state level) and prison and mental health records. If the license is approved, it is laminated and mailed to the applicant.

The new license is entered into the central computer, and local police departments routinely enter various court dispositions into the computer. If necessary because of such information, a license will be revoked. Even though the system is automated, it still takes around sixty days to get a license in Illinois. Once issued, however, the five-dollar license is good for five years.

MASSACHUSETTS

This state has three different forms, a "Firearms Identification Card," a "Permit to Purchase," and a "License to Carry" (Bartley-Fox), but since the last allows a person to purchase a handgun without either of the first two forms (and because the legal requirements are the same for the permit to purchase and the license to carry) nearly everyone in Massachusetts who wants to buy a handgun applies for a license to carry.

The applicant has to appear in person at his or her local police station for a photograph and to have fingerprints taken. Fees are set locally and run from $10 to $20, with certain exceptions, such as Boston, which charges $27.

Each police department then conducts whatever investigation it feels is necessary, and forwards the application to the State Department of Public Safety (DPS). DPS reviews the application and approves or disapproves. The approved license is then laminated and within one or two days is mailed back to the local police department which sends it to the applicant. Because the criminal records check takes much more time, some issued licenses are later revoked.

Records are kept manually, and there is no provision for canceling a license if the holder later becomes ineligible. Licenses, which expire on the holder's birthdate, are good for either four or five years.

A study of the Bartley-Fox law in Massachusetts by the Center for Applied Social Research at Northeastern University in Boston concluded that there was a significant decrease in the use of handguns in murders, assaults, and robberies as a result of the law. The Massachusetts law mandates a one-year jail term for carrying a handgun illegally.

According to the study, there was a 43 percent decline in handgun homicides in Boston during the period studied, while there was only an 11.1 percent decline in other similar-sized cities. The number of armed robberies in Massachusetts declined by 35.1 percent during 1975 and 1976, the first two years the law was in effect, while the number of armed robberies in the other forty-nine states declined by only 11.7 percent.

While there was an increase in the use of other weapons in Massachusetts during the period studied, the authors of the Northeastern report said the law's effect was socially desirable because "gun-related incidents are the most serious and injurious, so there has been a tendency toward less dangerous encounters."

"Particularly in the category of armed assaults, most of which typically stem from arguments and other spur-of-the-moment things," according to Dr. William J. Bowers, Director of the Northeastern Center and co-author of the study, "people seem less likely to run to their cars or their homes and come back with a gun. Instead, they appear to have just reached for a barstool or something more frequently.

"We don't see it as a deliberate substitution of a knife or some other weapon for a gun," he added, "but rather an emotional resort to whatever is handy during a heated conflict, with guns being less handy because of the law."

A similar license-to-carry law was passed in Connecticut in 1981 on the day the Pope was shot. Other states are now examining this approach.

CALIFORNIA

Anyone who wants to buy a handgun from a dealer in California must fill out an application known as a "Dealer's Record of Sale." The dealer sends a copy of the application to both the local police and the state Department of Justice, and then must wait fifteen days before turning over the weapon to the purchaser. At present, local police are not required to act on the application, but some of them do. The Department of Justice processes all applications and conducts a name check of state criminal records before the waiting period is over.

Dealers are notified to hold up the sale for one of two reasons: 1. ineligibility; or 2. the waiting period is almost over but the investigation is still going on. In all other cases, which include the great majority, the dealer is not notified. A computerized system is used for record-keeping. There is no fee, and there is no license, as such. A buyer must go through the same process for every gun purchased.

MARYLAND

This East Coast state has an "application of purchase" requirement. The dealer must send a copy of the application to the district state police office or, in the case of certain urban areas, to the city or county police. The dealer then has to wait seven days before transferring the weapon to the applicant. The police do a local records check and in most cases also a state check. (The state police are required by law to do this, and customarily the local police also do it.) Neither local nor state police have direct access to state criminal history records and must request a check from state police headquarters by phone or by Teletype. The police approve or disapprove the application and then return it to the dealer.

Unlike the California system, Maryland's dealers are notified in all cases, not just when the application is denied. The police review is usually not finished by the end of the seven-day waiting period (it normally takes ten to fifteen days) but most dealers, even though not required to do so by law, appear to wait until they are notified. Once the weapon is turned over to the applicant, the dealer sends the application to state police headquarters where it is filed manually. There is no fee.

NORTH CAROLINA

All individuals who wish to buy a handgun in North Carolina must get a "Permit to Purchase" from their county sheriff. Even though the law states that the sheriff must satisfy himself as to the applicant's good moral character, there are few formal requirements, and the system is completely decentralized. Different counties have different procedures as to waiting periods, record checks, and personal references. Photographs and fingerprints are not required, and records are kept only at the county level. This is the kind of state system that would be greatly improved by a federal handgun control law.

South Carolina has also acted in direct response to the handgun war. The experience of this state is particularly revealing. In the Charleston *News and Courier,* Keith Schneider gave a brief history:

> In 1901, South Carolina ratified the toughest law in the history of American handgun prohibitions—a statute banning pistol sales to all citizens except sheriffs and their special deputies. The law was designed to keep handguns out of the hands of blacks and recently

arrived immigrants, groups deemed by authorities to be dangerous to the public good . . .

For most of the twentieth century, the 1901 Act remained in effect, making the possession of a weapon less than 20 inches in length and less than three pounds an illegal act. But in 1965, after succumbing to heavy criticism from the National Rifle Association and thousands of gun proponents throughout the state, South Carolina repealed the 1901 Act and replaced it with one of the least restrictive gun laws in the nation. The new legislation required dealers to have state licenses. Buyers, though, were subject to very little scrutiny. If a buyer were old enough, looked straight and had the cash, he could buy as many handguns in South Carolina as he wished.

As a result, South Carolina emerged in the late 1960's and early 1970's as a major supplier of handguns to areas in the North and Midwest with much stricter controls. Even with passage of the 1968 Federal Gun Control Act, outlawing mail-order sales, military surplus sales, sales to convicted felons, and interstate sales of handguns and shotguns without special permission, South Carolina became known nationwide as a gun runner's haven. In 1973, the BATF conducted a detailed study of 16 major cities, cataloging where guns used in crimes were coming from. Project Identification pinpointed South Carolina as the No. 1 supplier of illegal handguns to New York City, the No. 2 supplier to Charlotte, N.C., and the No. 3 supplier to Philadelphia and Boston.

Consequently, in June 1975, the state legislature again enacted a somewhat more restrictive gun law prohibiting buyers from purchasing more than one handgun every thirty days. Under the new law, dealers and purchasers are required to fill out a detailed purchase and application record at the time of sale. Buyers are required to provide proof of residency—normally a driver's license—and must sign a statement swearing they are not convicted felons, mentally incompetent, drug addicts, fugitives, members of subversive organizations or habitual drunkards. Dealers must list gun type, caliber and serial number. One copy is given to buyers; one copy is kept by dealers; one copy is sent to state law-enforcement division headquarters in Columbia for entry into the agency's computer where facts are checked. Perjury can result in fines and jail sentences.

Two things happened when South Carolina toughened its gun

control laws. First, illegal shipments of guns from South Carolina to the North and Midwest dropped from a flood to a trickle. Last year BATF conducted a second study of illegal gun trafficking, and found South Carolina far down on the list in New York, Boston and Philadelphia. Says a BATF agent in New York: "South Carolina doesn't present a problem any more. Florida has taken the lead."

Most importantly, though, violent crime in South Carolina went down and the number of murders statewide dropped dramatically. For five years beginning in 1969, murder rates in South Carolina increased, with handgun murders leading the increase. In 1974, 452 people were murdered in South Carolina; 58 percent or 264 people were killed with handguns. The numbers declined only slightly in 1975. But in 1976, after the law had been in force for one year, murders dropped to 327, with handgun murders dropping to 147 or less than 45 percent. The total decline—125 murders—was almost entirely accounted for by the drop in handgun murders (117). Shotgun and knife murders, the most popular murder methods after handguns, remained steady.

Since the handgun menace is most pronounced in our urban areas, it is not surprising to see them taking the lead in handgun control. The successful passage of the New York mandatory sentencing law in August 1980 was in no small part due to the media's unprecedented focus on the problem in New York City, to Mayor Edward Koch's political leadership and the active involvement of many in the business community. Ironically, other cities have been unable to follow suit, handcuffed by their respective state legislatures by something known as "pre-emption." This denies cities the right to pass their own laws, under the claim that handgun control legislation is a matter that can only be acted on by the states themselves.

For example, the city of Philadelphia wanted to require a license or permit to purchase a gun with written notification of the purchase being sent to the chief of police. However, the state supreme court ruled it unconstitutional because the state legislature pre-empted the issue. In Atlanta, the secretary to the former governor, Carl Sanders, was shot and killed by an ex-mental patient who had easily acquired a Saturday Night Special at a pawnshop. When the Atlanta city council tried to act, they also ran into the pre-emption problem. In thirteen states, there is some kind of pre-emption law stopping cities and other localities from taking action to stem handgun carnage in their own communities.

Across America, cities are *trying* to do something about the handgun problem. But too often their efforts are hampered by such policies as state pre-emption or the existence of weak—or nonexistent—laws in neighboring states. Once again, the national situation cries out for a *federal* handgun-control law.

EDITORIAL OPINION

In this chapter on American opinion and law, I would be remiss if I failed to mention the support that the handgun control movement has received from the editorial pages of papers across the nation. Some of these papers have supported the movement for its entire life.

As a group, American editorial writers have done a great deal to keep the cause of handgun control before the American public. Their support is not confined to certain areas of the country only, or to just the large cities. Here is a sampling of what papers across the country had to say both before and after the shooting of President Reagan.

Today's Metro section is a grim yearbook, a compendium of 175 local tragedies with a single cause of death: guns. Those gun-worshippers who still blather about how people, not guns, kill people, might well consider whether they themselves aren't accessories—because their campaign to keep those guns and bullets coming is clearly endangering lives. As their bleat goes on, the gun traffic flows and the lives keep ending. Are they not responsible? . . . Until the members of Congress react seriously to these everyday deaths instead of giving lip service to "senseless killings" whenever a celebrity is murdered, guns—made, sold, stolen and shot by people—will keep on killing people.

Washington Post
December 31, 1980

The nation awoke yesterday still dazed from the surrealistic nightmare of its President gunned down on the streets of Washington . . . the United States simply must devise some ways to keep handguns out of the possession of those who would use them to kill and to maim. This conclusion, or something like it, has been reached many times before in the wake of some heinous attack on a national leader, but nothing ever seems to come of it. Mr. Reagan, ironically, counts himself among those who oppose gun control . . .

Arkansas Gazette
Little Rock
April 1, 1981

Almost before the smoke had cleared from the latest attempt to assassinate a president, renewed calls for sensible handgun control began clashing with even louder outcries from those who argue the right to keep and bear arms without restraint.

Of course we have lots of gun regulations. There are thousands of state and local gun control laws, some tough and some absurdly weak, in a crazy-quilt pattern across the land. And some clearly reduce gun-related crime. But overall their presence superficially strengthens the arguments of the gun lobby that gun laws do little or no good.

They won't do much good until we get serious enough to pass a sensible *national* gun control law.

Courier-Journal
Louisville, Kentucky
April 1, 1981

In our opinion, the fact that a handgun was used in the heinous attack on the President doesn't in itself provide a compelling reason for a crackdown on America's estimated 55 million handguns. But the fact that more than 20,000 Americans were murdered last year —most of them by handguns—does.

That very increase of violent crime is what spurs thousands of people to buy handguns for self-defense. Many of these new gun owners lack the training to use their weapons effectively, but no one can challenge the sincerity of their concerns.

Still, the very accessibility of these weapons creates a problem. Is there no way to crimp the armed criminal without also curbing the law-abiding gun owner?

The answer may be suggested in a bumper sticker sported by opponents of gun-control measures: "When guns are outlawed, only outlaws will have guns." What is needed is something that reverses that effect, that constricts only criminals. And registration—not confiscation—would do just that . . .

In the past, unfortunately, the National Rifle Association and

other anti-gun control groups have opposed even registration,
mostly fearing that it would be a "first step" to banning handguns.

The better place to draw the line is by accepting registration
of handguns while opposing registration of rifles and shotguns.
In fact, the NRA and other legitimate groups should be encouraged
to improve their image by taking a role in a reasonable
program, helping legal owners protect their weapons and use
them safely.

Denver Post
April 9, 1981

Again the declarations of faith that try to pass for arguments, the
opponents of the deadly little handgun can only offer a few points
of reasoned observation.

Yes, but the fewer deadly weapons there are, the fewer people
will use them.

Yes, handguns are used to kill in places that have tough gun
control laws, but a national law making the ownership of handguns
illegal would reduce the flow from jurisdiction to jurisdiction.

Yes, the person bent on assassination will find his weapon; it may
be that gun control will more effectively reduce the shootings of
common citizens than of Presidents. Is that then an argument
against control? . . .

No, a national law making handguns illegal except for
law-enforcement authorities would not eliminate the vast stock of
these weapons in this decade or this century. But it would be a
beginning, a legacy to the grandchildren of this century in the hope
that their generation will be free of the plague of injury and death
that afflicts this one.

Los Angeles Times
April 1, 1981

AMERICA'S AVERAGE KIND OF DAY

"The day the President was shot," says an ad of Handgun Control,
Inc. in newspapers across the country, "was an average kind of day"
—meaning that more than 50 Americans were killed with
handguns. The gun lobby, led by the National Rifle Association, says
people kill, not guns. Polls show that most people disagree, but not
enough care to argue. So the nation fails to respond to an epidemic
of handgun deaths, unlike its strong reaction to the rash of deaths
from toxic shock syndrome and Legionnaires' disease.

Handguns accounted for almost half the homicides in the United
States in 1979. In fact, murder is the only cause of death in America

that is increasing, according to Reynolds Farley of the University of Michigan's Population Studies Center, who recently completed a study of homicide. The United States can slow down or prevent deaths from cancer, heart disease and tuberculosis, but it cannot seem to do anything about the rising rate at which people kill each other.

The rising homicide rate has many causes, but according to Professor Farley the major one is simply the increasing availability of firearms. The problem feeds on itself. As more and more people grow fearful of violence, they buy handguns for protection. The Treasury Department said there were 55 million in civilian hands in 1978. With more than two million added each year, the number today is probably close to 60 million.

Yet law-enforcement experts believe that a handgun in the home is virtually useless as protection against crime. More often than not, it is when the victim reaches for or displays a gun that the criminal is provoked to shoot.

The attempt on President Reagan's life has led to the introduction of bills to tighten handgun controls and stiffen penalties for their illegal use. Will anything be done? Senator Edward Kennedy and Representative Peter Rodino have introduced legislation that would allow gun sales only through licensed dealers, limit each buyer to two firearms in a year and require purchasers to be screened for criminal records and mental health. It is a modest proposal and should be enacted.

But unless the people who say they favor stricter gun controls are willing to say and do much more, tomorrow, too, will be an average kind of day.

New York Times
April 14, 1981

6
MR. SHIELDS
GOES TO
WASHINGTON

BY the beginning of 1975, the year after Nick was shot, I was able to see that the next few years of my life were probably going to be spent in the fight for handgun control. I didn't think then that my identification with the issue would become so complete or that my association would be so long-lasting. All I knew for sure was that I had to become part of the team that was fighting for handgun laws.

Besides educating myself on the facts of the handgun issue, I had to learn more about the entire legislative process.

I had a head start on most Americans because I knew who my congressman and senators were. Every year in Washington our representatives spend our taxes, but a large percentage of our nation's voters haven't the foggiest idea who *their* own representatives are! In the Senate, there are 100 members, two for each state. In the House of Representatives, there are 435 members, each representing a congressional district with a population of some 450,000 citizens. These are the players in the passage of any new legislation.

What I quickly found out was that the odds were heavily stacked on the side of the opposition. It can be very difficult for a controversial piece of legislation to pass the U.S. Congress. There are many, many ways for the pistol lobby to derail any handgun control bill.

A bill usually enters the legislative process when either a senator or congressman deposits the bill in a "hopper," which is a box in the Senate or House chamber. Once the bill is introduced, it is assigned a number: in the House, "H.R.＿＿," and in the Senate, "S.＿＿." The parliamentarian of the House or Senate receives the bill and refers it to the committee with jurisdiction over the substance of the bill. (Handgun control legislation is handled by the Senate and House Judiciary Committees.) The committee chairman then may or may not assign the bill to a subcommittee. For example, on the House side a handgun control bill would be referred to the House Judiciary Subcommittee on Crime. If a bill is going to die, it usually dies at the committee or subcommittee level.

The subcommittee provides a forum where the bill is likely to receive its most thorough consideration. Hearings are called on the measure in order to allow witnesses to testify for or against it. Included in the hearings are spokesmen from the federal agency affected by this particular bill.

After hearings are held, the subcommittee holds "mark-up" sessions. During these meetings, congressmen review each section of the bill and, in light of the testimony heard, constituent response, and their own views, decide to keep the suggested language or offer amendments or deletions. If the bill is then approved by a majority vote, the bill goes up to the full committee. There it may again be "marked-up." Once approved by the full committee, it can go to the Senate or House floor.

To get to the House floor, bills must first be cleared by the Rules Committee. This committee sets the guidelines for debate of measures going to the House floor. Besides setting a time limit for the debate, the committee can decide on a "closed," "modified," or "open" rule. If a closed rule is decided on, no amendments (changes) can be made to the bill on the floor. Under a modified or open rule, some changes can be offered.

If the House or Senate passes the bill, it is then sent to the other chamber and again referred to the appropriate committee. If the committee approves the bill, it goes to the floor, where it must be approved. Seldom does a bill passed by the House contain exactly the same language or provisions as a bill passed by the Senate (and vice versa). When there are differences in the language, the bill goes to a "conference," where representatives from the Senate and House meet to reconcile the differences. Once a final form of the bill is agreed on, it goes back to both the House and Senate for approval.

The bill is then sent to the White House for presidential action. If the President signs it, it becomes law. If he vetoes the bill, it can only be passed if two-thirds of the Senate and the House still agree to the measure. This is called "overriding the veto."

There are two ways of taking a vote in Congress: 1. by voice vote (ayes and nays), where the presiding officer in the House or Senate says the bill passed or failed according to the loudness of the voices; 2. by a roll-call vote in which each congressman or senator's vote is carefully recorded.

That, in a nutshell, is the legislative system. Each Congress meets for a two-year period during which some 20,000 bills may be introduced, with only 5 percent becoming law. And if a bill fails in one Congress, it has to begin again at step one in the next.

By late 1975, both Handgun Control and Pete Shields had a long way to go. I was somewhat familiar with the handgun issue, and understood the difficulties facing any handgun control legislation. But there were a number of fundamental questions still to be decided. What legislation would we lobby for? And who, exactly, were "we"? What organization was needed? Whom did we represent? What were our goals and what strategies would, could, or should we employ to accomplish them? There was much to do.

Those of us in Handgun Control, Inc. were an odd but interesting team back in 1975 when we first got started on this campaign. First there was Mark Borinsky, the young Ph.D. in psychology, whose experience as a holdup victim had been the catalyst for the organization; next was Ed Welles, retired from the Central Intelligence Agency, who knew the way things were supposed to work in Congress; and then there was Charlie Orasin, a young Georgetown University graduate, from New York State, who'd already seen more of the internal workings of politics—first as a congressional aide and then as a campaign aide to former Senator Javits of New York—than the rest of us put together.

Those were just the most visible and on-the-scene personalities. Holding the organization together at that crucial stage were a number of essential volunteers and a dedicated board of directors which included police chiefs, congressmen, and leaders of local handgun control groups.

What we were trying to do was to start a grass-roots "citizens lobby"-type organization that would bring the voice of the people to the debate on how to control handgun violence. But our main problem was that we did not yet know how to do that.

Hindsight is a wonderful thing, but it often blurs reality. I'd like to be able to say that we all sat down and intelligently plotted the future of Handgun Control, Inc. (then called the National Council to Control Handguns), in a careful step-by-step progression that led us to our present position—a paid membership of 150,000, and at least twice that many known supporters. But that is not exactly the way it happened. We have had more than our share of false starts, ups-and-downs, and occasional strolls down the garden path.

You read so often of the "powers-that-be" in this country putting their money and prestige behind various causes. Why, with the killings of the famous and not-so-famous, hadn't a Handgun Control, Inc. been founded many years earlier?

The answer is that no rich "fat cat" came to the door and said, "Here is $100,000; start a lobby." From the beginning, we were a boot-strap organization, always wondering if we had enough money to pay the rent and the meager salaries. Mark had the most familiarity with what we had to do. He was the first to mention the concept of direct mail, by which you find—through the careful culling of rented mailing lists—the names of people likely to support your cause. If you received one membership check in return for every hundred letters you sent out, that was a high yield. But that single donor became a reliable source of funds for your cause. And when multiplied by many hundreds, at a $15 annual rate, you had a foundation of financial support. The problem was getting the seed money to start this process.

I wrote to those on my Christmas card list seeking financial support for the organization. Other members of the board did likewise. The response was, considering the non-professionalism of our approach, very good. But that exhausted our main resource;

you can only ask the same people for money so often.

We realized that it was time to turn to the pros, not just for fund-raising advice, but regarding the whole concept of starting and running a grass-roots lobby.

During our early years, we were fortunate to receive free professional advice from handgun control supporters in Washington. The top Washington law firms, Covington and Burling, and Wilmer, Cutler and Pickering treated us as "pro bono publico" (for the public good) clients. These firms helped in developing the legal structure of the organization and eventually its legislative strategy. Now we enjoy the added help of Fried, Frank, Harris, Shriver and Kampelman.

Several people recommended that we call Roger Craver and Tom Mathews, two political consultants who'd been around Washington for a while and whose backgrounds included such well-known enterprises as the Peace Corps and Common Cause, the first grass-roots citizens lobby of the modern era. We did so, and they have been associated with our organization ever since. (Tom Mathews, a breath of fresh air in a town too often populated with overly serious people, calls himself "Chinkagook," meaning that he is my guide through the sometimes treacherous wilderness of behind-the-scenes Washington.)

What was so pleasing about Roger Craver and Tom Mathews was that they did not treat us as just another client who needed consulting expertise. That they truly believed in our cause was apparent from our first meeting.

In early 1975, Tom and Roger advised us that the best way for us to develop a sound financial base and to enhance our public and legislative credibility was to launch an aggressive membership development campaign. Tom, especially, sensed that the time was ripe to recruit a massive citizen force for handgun control. He and Roger prepared a detailed proposal that called for our fledgling group to spend something like $50,000 "up front" for a big and bold direct-mail campaign.

When I told them that we didn't have that kind of money, and that we couldn't afford their fee, they said they would "put it on the cuff," and that we could pay them back a little at a time as the membership grew and funds became available. I said we would have to think about it.

A short time later, I told Roger and Tom we just could not do it; we could not commit the organization to so grand and ambitious a plan. The whole idea went against my conservative grain, and the other directors agreed. We would push forward on a more modest basis. (With the benefit of hindsight, I'm not sure that was the wisest decision.)

Money, and how to raise it, was only one of our concerns at that early stage. Another was a central question of organizational philosophy: What were we *for?* Would we go all the way and call for a total ban on handguns, or would we support something less, such as registration and licensing? It was not a simple question.

Almost everyone who loses someone to the American Handgun War—mother, father, spouse, brother, sister, or other relative or friend—reacts to the loss by wanting an immediate cure. You feel the need for an instant solution, a magic wand you can wave over the problem and make it disappear. One such magic wand is the concept of a total ban on the sale and possession of handguns, especially those of the Saturday Night Special variety. Almost all victims, and I was no exception, go through a period in which they feel the need for a total ban.

There is, however, as previously mentioned, a serious problem with the total ban approach: The American people do not support the idea. Nonetheless, in the early days of our organization we supported the Hart-Bingham bill, a bill that would restrict the possession of handguns to the military, law-enforcement officials, licensed security guards, and licensed pistol clubs. The bill was drawn from a legislative recommendation of the 1968 Eisenhower Commission on the Causes and Prevention of Violence. But, even as we supported the bill, I was beginning to move away from what I feared was an inflexible and unworkable position.

Coincidentally, at the time I was going through this change of attitude, President Ford's Attorney General Edward Levi testified that there might be some validity in the idea of a two-step system —the concept of having strict controls on sale and possession, in large cities with high crime rates and a large number of handguns in circulation, but less stringent controls for small towns and rural areas where there wasn't as much crime and not so many handguns.

I thought that approach made a great deal of sense, both practically and politically. Let those people in big cities have the strict controls they want, and in the more rural areas where fewer people want them, let's not impose them. The more I thought about it, the more I liked the idea. The Ford Administration had floated the idea—a time-honored Washington way of testing the reaction to a legislative idea before actually proposing the legislation. Although we had already come out in favor of the Hart-Bingham bill, I asked our lawyers to review the Levi proposal. Their analysis indicated the approach would create significant federal involvement in local areas. At the same time, since the regional application of the controls was to be triggered by high crime rates, many of the cities affected would be in the South, which severely undercut the political acceptability of the approach.

With increasing legislative attention to the handgun issue came increased press coverage. And more of it came our way. The publicity of my involvement with Handgun Control, Inc. evolved initially from the efforts of Carl Spitzer, a public-relations specialist. Carl told a reporter from the *New York Daily News* that there "might be a story in this guy Shields who quit a big corporate job to work for handgun control after his own son was killed." Suddenly, there I was one Sunday morning, written up in the paper with the largest circulation in the country.

That article in turn fueled other articles, both about my involvement and the work of our organization. A continuing series of interviews began to bring us recognition and, we hoped, some credibility. But despite all the attention we still faced the problem of how to finance and build an organization. We had a kind of tacit agreement that in order for us to be minimally effective we needed 100,000 members.

I'm not sure, however, that we fully grasped what this meant. When, in 1976, we reached the 5,000 level for the first time, we were exultant. Five thousand times the membership fee of $15 meant $75,000. That was a staggering sum compared to the meager budgets we'd been working with.

And each time the membership rose in significant increments we felt a similar surge of excitement and renewed hope. I think we were more encouraged by the continuing growth than we were by the prospect that one day we might reach the magic number of 100,000 members.

Meanwhile there was some internal debate as to whether or not we really needed that many members to be effective. The debate became our own version of the chicken-versus-the-egg problem. Which came first, the membership or the influence?

Should we concentrate on building the membership as fast as possible and then go up to Capitol Hill and say, "Look, we have 100,000 members so you have to listen to us!" Or should we go to the Hill with our position papers and then report back to the membership—and the prospective members—that we already had some influence on the Congress?

It is a Washington truth that, when it comes to lobbying, you have to *look* like somebody before you can *be* somebody. We soon learned what that meant. As sincere and dedicated as our people were, we had to give the appearance of having clout in order to gain new members, because gaining new members would eventually give us real clout. So, when we got written up in *People* magazine and the *New Yorker,* we had the articles reproduced by the thousands. We then sent out the reprints with our requests for new members, which helped greatly. We were learning the ropes of modern Washington.

At about the same time, we designed a direct-mail package which included a brochure and a letter signed by me. The letter simply outlined my story of handgun violence, the growing violence across the country, and urged people to join together to win this fight.

One key obstacle we had to overcome was the development of a "letterhead." By this I don't mean our name and address, but a list of people who supported us with their time or talents or simply their names. As articles appeared about our work, we sent copies to well-known Americans who we thought supported handgun control. Some of those who have publicly backed us include:

Steve Allen	Hal Holbrook
Arthur Ashe	Mayor Maynard Jackson
Marjorie Benton	Albert Jenner, Jr.
Leonard Bernstein	Dr. Martin Luther King, Sr.
Edmund G. Brown, Sr.	Ann Landers
Ellen Burstyn	Edward Levi
Julia Child	John Lindsay

Milton Eisenhower	Marsha Mason
Mayor Dianne Feinstein	Patrick Murphy
Mayor Kenneth Gibson	William Ruckelshaus
Mayor Richard Hatcher	Neil Simon
Mayor Janet Gray Hayes	Roy Wilkens

Their credibility helped us attract more and more members.

Ours was not, however, a nice, neat, linear progression upward. We grew in steps and in spurts, but to us each new plateau, each increment of one thousand new members, was an event as exciting as the first one-thousand increment had been. I, personally, have never been able to get over the feeling of pride and awe at the growth of our membership.

When I went into the fight for handgun control initially, I don't believe I set any time limits. I didn't say, "I will give this two years, or five or ten years." However, I do know that I did *not* tell myself that I would be spending the rest of my working days with the organization. Yet that now appears to be what has happened, for I have come to see what kind of time it takes to build an effective organization based on an active and vocal constituency able to convince the Congress. The hard part is created by the highly emotional and controversial nature of our message. Congressmen have no desire to face such issues (like abortion and school busing) unless they absolutely have to because the public demands it.

It has become axiomatic on Capitol Hill and around Washington to say that you can't pass handgun control legislation in an even numbered year—because those are the years in which national elections are held. I am not sure if I believe that axiom, especially in light of the increased numbers of voters who tell pollsters they want some form of handgun control, but that was one of the reasons why 1975 was such an active year in Congress for this issue.

That Congress, the 94th, was considered one of the most liberal to be seated. Many members had ridden into office on the crest of the Watergate wave which drowned so many Republicans. Congressman John Conyers of Michigan, the chairman of the House Judiciary Subcommittee on Crime, decided to hold a series of unprecedented hearings on the handgun question. Those were the hearings I began to attend (on my vacation days off from Du

Pont) with Ed Welles. Hearings would also be held that year in the Senate in both the Judiciary and Government Operations Committees. During the course of the hearings, hundreds of handgun-control bills were introduced.

Five presidential commissions had called for restrictive handgun control legislation and Americans were being killed at a record rate, yet nothing had been done. If any Congress was to come to grips with the handgun carnage, we felt, it would certainly be the 94th.

A quick political lesson: In 1972, after George Wallace was shot, Senator Birch Bayh held a series of hearings on the handgun issue. A moderate handgun control bill was passed by the Senate by the wide margin of 68-25. But the House failed to take it up. They had no desire to do so in an even-numbered year. As a result of his Senate bill, the gun zealots went after Birch Bayh in his 1974 reelection bid. Although he was reelected, he wanted to make sure that next time the House took the first step. Nothing angers a senator or congressman more than being forced to take a tough stand on a controversial issue which other members manage to avoid.

So 1975 saw the historic Conyers hearings. The hearings were held not only in Washington, but in selected cities across the country. We had the opportunity to testify twice before Conyers' subcommittee, and testified in support of the Hart-Bingham approach. The hearings demonstrated broad-based support for handgun control legislation. The Conyers hearings began in March and continued through early October. Eight volumes of testimony were taken. In June, President Ford sent a moderate handgun control bill to the Congress. Ironically, he had a hard time finding a senator or congressman to introduce his bill! Finally, Senator Hiram Fong of Hawaii and Congressman Robert McClory of Illinois introduced the bill as a courtesy. Three months later, two attempts were made on President Ford's life, by Sarah Jane Moore and Squeaky Fromme. Both would-be assassins used handguns. The word spread that Ford would sign the toughest handgun bill Congress would pass.

Suddenly, there was great pressure on Conyers and his subcommittee to mark-up a bill and get it moving on the House side. Bayh had started moving a handgun control bill through his subcommittee, but was keeping close tabs on House progress.

Then came the logjam. Chairman Conyers introduced his bill, which would virtually ban all handguns. The ranking Republican on the subcommittee, Robert McClory, offered a more moderate licensing bill. Mr. Conyers preferred that his bill be the vehicle for the mark-up. It was summarily voted on and defeated. Not wanting to accept the McClory bill as an alternative, Mr. Conyers urged the subcommittee to draft an entirely new bill, and in the process review all alternative features subject by subject: licensing; registration; Saturday Night Specials; penalties; and so forth. This process was followed—much to the anger of Robert McClory and the delight of the pistol lobby. One gun lobbyist wanted to hold a testimonial dinner for Conyers! Marking-up a bill in this fashion is very time-consuming; the legislative calendar in the odd year of 1975 was quickly passing.

Finally, in November, under considerable pressure from the House leadership, the subcommittee reported out a modest bill. It was understood that ample time would be given to consider the bill in the full committee. A few weeks later, Senator Bayh's subcommittee approved a handgun control bill. As 1976, an election year, approached, the stage was actually set for passage of a handgun control bill.

In February, the House Judiciary Committee began consideration of the subcommittee bill. We made it known that we intended to continue supporting the idea of a total ban, and as a result we got our first hard lesson in the political facts of life.

The powers-that-be in the House Judiciary Committee (and, as a matter of fact, those on the Senate side too) called us in and read us the riot act. In effect, they said, "What's the matter with you people? Now, for the first time in modern history, we have a chance to pass *some* form of handgun control legislation, and you threaten the whole thing by holding out for a position that is unwinnable because it is politically unrealistic."

It was, as Charlie Orasin recalls it, like throwing cold water on a bunch of zealots.

Chastened, we agreed to go along with the bill that the House Judiciary Committee now appeared ready to approve and send on to the full House for a vote. A last-minute development that caused us to feel better about our compromise was the passage, by a vote of 18 to 14, of an amendment offered by Congressman Martin Russo, an Illinois Democrat, that would have prohibited the manufacture of a large percentage of handguns by redefining the "non-sporting" handgun, commonly called a Saturday Night Special.

The bill was now set for final approval, the farthest any gun control measure had ever progressed in the United States House of Representatives since 1968. We were ecstatic.

That weekend, while we enjoyed what we viewed as a special victory for handgun control forces, the National Rifle Association —about whom we'd heard so much, but whom we'd yet to see in performance—roared into action. All weekend long the NRA's computers hummed, printing up, addressing, and mailing the letters that urged their members to let Congress know how they felt about this threat to freedom, this attempt to limit an American's "constitutional right to bear arms."

Here's a sample:

DEAR NRA MEMBER

THE HOUSE JUDICIARY COMMITTEE IS MOVING QUICKLY TOWARD FINAL APPROVAL OF HR 11193 THE FEDERAL FIREARMS ACT OF 1976. CONTRARY TO WHAT THE MEDIA HAS REPORTED HR 11193 IS ONE OF THE STRONGEST ANTI-GUN BILLS EVER TO BE CONSIDERED BY THE CONGRESS. THE BILL WOULD OUTLAW THREE-QUARTERS OF ALL HANDGUNS NOW MANUFACTURED OR IMPORTED AND BAN THE SALE OR INHERITANCE OF MILLIONS ALREADY IN PRIVATE HANDS. THE BILLS RESTRICTIONS ON DEALERS ALSO WILL SEVERELY LIMIT AVAILABILITY OF ALL LONG GUNS AS WELL AS AMMUNITION. THE JUDICIARY COMMITTEE MEETS AGAIN THURSDAY, FEBRUARY 26, 1976. YOUR CONGRESSMAN, THE HONORABLE   PHONE
          IS ON THIS COMMITTEE. PLEASE TELEPHONE OR WIRE HIM IMMEDIATELY AND URGE HIM TO VOTE AGAINST HR 11193. ALSO GET YOUR FRIENDS TO CONTACT HIM TO VOTE AGAINST HR 11193.

HARLON B. CARTER
EXECUTIVE DIRECTOR

The mailgram was misleading. Congressman Russo called a press conference to explain how his amendment would *not* severely limit availability of all long guns as well as ammunition.

But the damage had already been done. Key members of the House Judiciary Committee received a flood of mailgrams and numerous phone calls. By midweek, we began to get word of the force and effectiveness of the pistol lobby's efforts. By Thursday, the day set to approve the bill, the pistol lobby had changed the votes of four committee members, Thomas Railsback (R-Ill.), George Danielson (D-Calif.), Henry Hyde (R-Ill.) and Edward Pattison (D-N.Y.). Danielson reportedly received 300 telegrams and phone calls from members of the NRA, and Patterson 400.

However, the pistol lobby couldn't change the bill. Its only recourse was to "kill" it by having it recommitted to the subcommittee. That's the word it passed down, and the bill was recommitted.

Even then the bill was not dead. A backlash developed against those who recommitted the bill. A moderate bill was hurriedly sent back to the full committee and passed on April 13, 20-12.

The bill now had to go to the House Rules Committee so that a rule for the debate could be set. While pending there, we heard of a meeting held with the House-Senate leadership—Carl Albert and Senator Mike Mansfield. At the meeting, Mansfield told Albert that even if the House passed the bill, the Senate would not act on it. After all, it was an election year. We leaked the story to the press. Mansfield denied he ever said it. But the bill died then and there. No House action was ever scheduled.

7
THE COMING
OF AGE

THE death of the handgun control bill in the 94th Congress was my legislative baptism of fire. I learned firsthand the difficulties legislation faced and I came to appreciate the lobbying prowess of the pistol lobby.

For the most part, 1976 was a bad year. Not only did we lose a handgun control opportunity on the national level, we were also startled by the defeat at the polls of the Massachusetts referendum. The most liberal state had voted down an admittedly very tough handgun control proposal.

The one bright ray of hope in 1976 was the election of the Democrats' dark-horse candidate, former Georgia governor Jimmy Carter. We had watched with amazement as he dispatched his opponents in the primaries and then edged out President Ford in the general election.

For the first time in our nation's history, the handgun issue surfaced during the course of the presidential debate. The candidates were asked their positions during one of the televised debates. President Ford, the target of two assassination attempts, reversed himself on the issue. Despite having sent a handgun control bill to the Congress in 1975, he now announced a position against new controls. *Coincidentally,* in September 1976, the National Rifle Association took the unprecedented step of endorsing a candidate for president—Gerald Ford.

Jimmy Carter's initial mention of his handgun-control stand was in the Florida primary, against George Wallace. His campaign promise: "I favor registration of handguns, a ban on the sale of cheap handguns, reasonable licensing provisions including a waiting period and prohibition of ownership by anyone convicted of a crime involving a gun and by those not mentally competent."

The statement was in line with the bill that had passed the House Judiciary Committee in the previous Congress.

After his election, we read that Mr. Carter was not just in favor of gun controls, he might even be *militant* on the issue. In an interview with *New Times* magazine, Carter's top aide Hamilton Jordan, in referring to the pro-gun lobby, said, "We're going to get those bastards."

And what a *model* leader for handgun control Jimmy Carter appeared to be. He was, or had been, a Southerner, a military officer, a hunter, a businessman, and a conservative! He seemed almost too good to be true.

Given our 1976 experience, we knew that if we were to be successful in 1977, we'd have to move a handgun control bill quickly, and that presidential leadership would be the key. So, based on the statements of Jordan and the President, we promptly sent a letter to the White House offering our support on the issue. We received a most encouraging letter from Hamilton Jordan, directing us to meet with key principals in the Justice Department.

I called them and asked for a meeting. At our initial session, they laid down the first commandment: The Carter Administration would do nothing on the handgun issue unless the handgun control forces were united behind it. These legislative planners and draftsmen were, for the most part, holdovers from the Ford Administration and they had watched in agony as what might have been the best chance for handgun control in their time slipped away. Basically, what they were telling me was that we would have to work together or not at all.

We agreed to back them, and they welcomed us into their confidence.

The strategy? To support a handgun control bill similar to the measure passed by the House Judiciary Committee, but especially tailored to the President's campaign promise.

Senator Kennedy, by then Chairman of the Senate Judiciary Committee, was a handgun control partisan. He could hold the bill for full committee action, thus circumventing the "Bayh problem." We felt that Congressman Peter Rodino, chairman of the House Judiciary Committee, should lead the fight on the House side. He had done an admirable job in marking-up the bill in the previous Congress.

In sum, the plan was to have a Carter handgun control bill offered by Senator Kennedy and Congressman Rodino. With the President and the leaders of the respective committees behind it, the bill could move quickly. The timetable was set to have the bill moving by April—early in an odd-numbered year!

By the time 1977 had barely started, we knew it was going to be a very busy—and, we hoped, successful—year. In 1976, while we were getting our legislative baptism by fire in the 94th Congress and watching Jimmy Carter astound the pros by winning the Democratic nomination and then the presidency, I had initiated the formulation of a basic "marketing plan" for handgun control.

I had been a marketing manager for over ten years, and knew that the successful marketing of consumer products required well-thought-out plans with detailed strategies for accomplishing each step. A similar process was involved in the successful selling of a candidate to the voters—as Jimmy Carter proved. Why not use the same methods to sell a legislative concept to Congress?

So, in 1975 I spent a lot of time searching out and meeting Washington's best political strategists and planners. Of course, as almost anyone with even a grain of political savvy would have known, the best ones of both parties were already working double-time for their respective '76 candidates. So, although I made contacts, actual work on our plan had to wait until after November '76. Actually, I should say until after November 1, because during that first week of November, about two days before the election, I received a surprise call from one of those always-on-the-go, ultra-busy political strategists.

He said, "Pete, you asked for my help some time ago, and I had to turn you down because I was so busy. Well, with only two days to go, I've done about all I can for my candidate, so give me a week's vacation and I'm ready to start on handgun control."

He knew we didn't have the money to pay his normal fees, but, like so many of the real Washington pros I've been fortunate to meet and work with, his ideals and commitment were not sacrificed to the demands of practical economics.

By early 1977, we were working hard, with the best in the business from both parties, on a professional plan for achieving an effective national handgun control law in this country. This plan covered all aspects of our job: membership development; organization building; fund-raising; polling; legislation and legislative action; "constituency motivation" and grass-roots lobbying; political action; and political realities. Again, I have to mention the sincere commitment to our cause by all our advisors: That kind of plan would have cost a political candidate $50,000 to $100,000. We were charged $10,000.

The central concept around which our entire plan was built has been vitally important to our growth. (I almost said "success," but I will not use that word until we get an effective national handgun control law in this country.) That central concept, or idea, is the reason I got through to my congressman so easily, the reason I was able to corral such top-flight consultants, and the reason Mark Borinsky and Ed Welles brought me into the organization in the first place—*my victim status.*

As one of our political strategists put it, early on, "Pete, if you are going to Washington as a committed activist with a business background, you can certainly help; but if you're also coming as a father who is willing to go public with his tragedy, who's willing to make it America's tragedy, then you can make a tremendous difference!"

I was willing. That conversation was the beginning of what we would come to call our "victims strategy," which today pervades all our plans, strategies, and organizational thinking.

In 1977, the victims strategy was woven into all aspects of the plan, which, when it was all finished, became a three-volume tome.

Our executive committee immediately recognized its value, despite its size (and cost!), and approved the plan for testing as a blueprint for raising money. So, besides working with the administration and the Justice Department on legislation, we were now working to raise money for, and to test out, our basic plan of attack.

Our first step was to get important political endorsements of our plan to assure potential financial supporters we knew what we were talking about. This came more easily than I expected, which reassured me that the plan was sound. Congressmen Peter Rodino and John Anderson, and Senators Jacob Javits and Ted Kennedy all wrote letters of support endorsing the plan which we immediately incorporated into the "executive summary" we showed potential backers.

The next step was what would become a continuing fund-raising and public-information campaign. In reality, this was a sales job. We had to sell not only the need for handgun control, but we also had to sell ourselves and our plan for achieving it. Regardless of a person's commitment to a cause, no one wants to give to a losing effort or a lost cause.

This meant expanding our then modest direct-mail efforts into a major campaign. But that, as we had come to know so well, would take seed money. So one of our major efforts during 1977 was a series of meetings around the country at which we would give a twenty-minute pitch to audiences of twenty-five to a hundred potential donors—just like raising money for a political candidate.

For these meetings our consultants insisted on a slide show. Communication of an emotional subject, they said, is best done visually. The first of what would eventually be several shows was developed and taken on the road.

Though fund-raising and membership development were the primary purposes of the slide presentations, we put them on anywhere we could get an audience. Among the first to see the show were my friends and neighbors in Wilmington. John O'Hear, rector of our church—and close personal friend—asked me to speak at Christ Church, our parish for almost thirty years and the church from which Nick had been buried.

As I looked out at all the faces, I was nervous. This was not something I felt at all comfortable doing. I knew two things about that audience: 1. They sympathized with me and my family; and 2. They did not necessarily believe in gun control.

I began by telling them that I felt both humble and nervous:

> . . . Humble because so many of you, and other Wilmington friends of the Shields', have supported my efforts so generously. All I can

say tonight is to repeat my heartfelt and sincere appreciation for both your philosophical and monetary support. Your initial and continued support has made the National Council to Control Handguns the viable and effective organization it is today. Without it we wouldn't exist.

Nervous because I have a gut feeling that some of you have done so out of friendship for the Shields rather than out of true conviction as to the rightness of my stands on handgun control. Now, I'm here to share with you the specific positions you are espousing by supporting Pete Shields and the National Council to Control Handguns. I hope you leave with the same conviction that you've shown to date. I suspect, however, that some may leave with more questions than conviction. Maybe the best I can hope for is that all of you will leave with a deeper understanding of the issue and a recognition of the social, ideological and personal trade-offs involved in its solution . . .

I then proceeded to lay out all the horrible statistics of gun violence, the beliefs and the programs of NCCH, and a refutation of the various arguments used by the NRA. I ended by telling them:

. . . Handgun control won't be easy and won't be painless. It would *inconvenience* the firearms industry, the target-shooter, the tin-can plunker, possibly even some hunters. But like all complex issues in a complex society, solutions must weigh the benefits versus the cost to both the individual and society. There is no such thing as a one-hundred-percent costless solution. All have their negatives for some people, their positives for others. Just as doing nothing has its opposite positives and negatives.

It's through this weighing process that I come out strongly on the side of strict federal control of concealable handguns. Again, not rifles and shotguns, as they're not concealable and not a significant factor in American violence. Just handguns—whose primary virtue is concealability; whose primary purpose is to kill people. To kill people in secret, with stealth and without getting caught.

I'm convinced that the vast majority of Americans, whether from the North, East, South, or West, agree and are seriously searching for a solution other than just fighting violence with more violence. I think they are now ready not only to passively acknowledge the need for handgun controls, but to start demanding it . . .

This was to be the first of many, many speeches and slide-show presentations I would make to people from all walks of life. In each case I would use the fact that I was a victim of handgun violence because we had to get across the fact that this is an emotional life-and-death issue, not just statistics.

There is one point about handgun violence that eventually reaches anyone whose mind is even partially open, and that is that they, or theirs, could be next. Certainly, the odds are in favor of handgun violence striking members of certain groups—the poor, the blacks, the less-educated, and most especially poor young black males—but *no one* can get a guarantee that it won't happen to them or to their loved ones.

Meanwhile, back at the Justice Department work proceeded on the handgun control bill. I was getting a bit anxious when by April the bill had not even been sent to the White House. During that month, the U.S. Conference of Mayors held a meeting devoted exclusively to handgun control, and some two dozen groups from all across the country met to discuss their local efforts. We felt that a little grass-roots lobbying was in order, so we asked for a meeting with the attorney general, and when he wasn't available an assistant attorney general agreed to meet with us. We presented a letter to the attorney general signed by all the group leaders, urging him to move on the Carter legislation. He told us it would be ready "soon." And it was. Our friends at the Justice Department called us to thank us for the "prodding," which had apparently been needed. The bill was quickly sent over to the White House for final approval.

Then, for the first time, we began to hear rumors that Jimmy Carter's White House was growing cool toward the idea of the bill. In an attempt to waylay our fears, we sought a meeting with Stuart Eizenstadt, the President's chief domestic policy advisor. We weren't able to get such a meeting, but his people told us not to worry, the Carter forces were still high on handgun control, but the bill could not be introduced until after the summer recess.

We decided it was time to focus some public attention on the Carter bill, as it was now June and apparently no one outside the administration, and certainly not the general public, knew there even was a Carter handgun control bill. So we leaked a copy of the bill to a well-respected newspaper. The front-page story that followed generated considerable *positive* editorial comment, but it did *not* succeed in getting the bill out of the White House.

The Congressional recess came (in August) and went, but we still got only promises and no action. As each day passed, so did hope of legislative activity. Finally, we were told that it would be introduced in September, but September passed and it was not. Then we were told October, but that too passed. Next, they said November, but that month also passed without the bill leaving the White House. Then we heard rumors again. The delay on the bill had to do with "a question of legislative priorities." We could appreciate this answer because the Carter Administration was at the time battling to come up with an acceptable energy package for the Hill.

When we asked about the bill in early 1978, we were told that the White House was now thinking about making it part of a larger crime package, and that the bills would probably not be introduced until April. We knew then that there would be no handgun control legislation passed in the 95th Congress.

Fortunately, we were keeping busy on other fronts. In 1977, we joined with the District of Columbia corporation counsel in beating back an effort by the NRA to have the courts overturn D.C.'s tough new handgun control law. That was a sweet, sweet victory over the NRA.

At the same time, we began closely examining an unused option: the regulatory power of the Treasury. The previous year, the Police Foundation Report had come out with many recommendations which could be implemented through regulation, as opposed to legislation or court action. We decided to see if we could prod the Treasury Department into taking a few steps. It turned out to be a very interesting and educational experience.

Our lawyers filed a technical procedure called a "Petition for Rule-Making," by which, in effect, we asked the Treasury Department to issue two new regulations: 1. to require licensed handgun manufacturers and dealers to report, promptly, the thefts or losses of handguns; and 2. to require them to take minimum security precautions to guard against theft. The Treasury Department responded by saying that they were working on a set of new regulations including one relating to thefts and losses, but didn't feel they had the authority to require security devices. We disagreed, took the latter issue to court, and (almost a year later) got a ruling that Treasury did have such authority.

In March 1978, Treasury issued their proposed regulations that would: 1. require each gun manufactured to have a unique serial number (to help police in tracing); 2. require the prompt reporting of thefts and losses; and 3. require reports to Treasury by each manufacturer and dealer as to the movement of guns within the commercial distribution channels—i.e., sales, receipts, transfers, losses, inventories, etc. This last regulation would give Treasury the authority to audit the gun pipeline and see where guns were leaking out to the criminal. Not surprisingly, the nation's police chiefs endorsed these regulations.

Earlier we had met with various Treasury Department officials to discuss both the Justice Department bill and the possibility of such regulations. One meeting was held with the legislative liaison for Treasury. Sitting in on the meeting was James Featherstone, Treasury's director of enforcement. It was a good meeting, and we left feeling optimistic.

We were in for a bad surprise. In Washington, one hears the term "revolving door" used to describe the situation when a government employee specializing in an important area leaves the government and then shows up almost the next day as an employee of or consultant to a private firm seeking government contracts in that very same area. I knew about the practice, but I'd never experienced its reality. At least not until we met Mr. Featherstone who, within a couple of months of our meeting, left Treasury and was immediately hired as the general counsel of the National Rifle Association! Featherstone had frequently met with the Carter people on the gun control issue, so there was much grumbling, suspicion, and even a few unpleasant rumors about what effect his new job might have on future efforts of the Carter Administration to "get those bastards." My education in the ways of Washington was continuing.

When the proposed Treasury Department regulations were made public, the fight began in earnest. Several pistol-lobby congressmen tried to undermine the department's credibility by suggesting that Treasury had secret plans already on the drawing board which outlined a massive registration plan for *all* guns and all gun owners.

The pistol lobby's attack was a massive effort, focusing on Richard Davis, then assistant secretary of the Treasury for Enforcement. As the *Washington Star* put it, in a series on handgun control:

> When the gun lobby had finished with him, Davis was summoned to Capitol Hill to be taught a lesson. Congress asked him how much it would cost to implement his proposal, he replied about $4.2 million and lawmakers then voted to cut the BATF budget by that amount.
>
> Davis said it was a classic case of NRA distortion. Under the Davis-BATF proposal, gun retailers—not the BATF—would keep the records containing the names and addresses of individual buyers, and thus the names of individual pistol owners would not be in government files. But by having the names of the retailers in its computers, BATF would be able to more easily trace firearms used in crimes.
>
> The proposed changes, Davis told a House subcommittee, would "involve only what Congress has authorized and what the public has a right to expect—that we seek ways to enforce our current laws more effectively."
>
> NRA computers spun out thousands of mailgrams to association members warning that the proposed regulations would "establish a computerized national registration system," and "would set the groundwork for the stated goal of President Carter and the Justice Department: registration of all private firearms."
>
> Neal Knox, the NRA's chief lobbyist, told reporters at the time that the issue provided the NRA an opportunity to fire a warning shot over the head of the Carter Administration.
>
> "It never hurts to further Mr. Carter's education," Knox said then . . .

It was the last time the Carter Administration ever raised the issue of gun control with the Congress.

8
ANSWERING "THE OTHER SIDE"

WE would have handgun control in this country today were it not for two factors—a confused and divided public, and the largely overrated clout of the pistol lobby.

Not only does the American public know that criminal violence is growing at an epidemic rate, it also knows that handguns play a major role in that growth. But people are confused. What is the best way to achieve personal and public safety? Handgun laws? Stiffer criminal laws? More police? Owning a handgun oneself?

Where people live makes a great difference in how they view the problem of handgun violence and the issue of control. There is a *major* division in the thinking and lifestyle of our rural and our urban populations, a difference that too often pits what people perceive to be the private rights and freedoms of the smaller, rural population against the "societal" rights and fears of our larger, urban population.

What worries the people in the rural areas is the possibility that handgun control measures are the first step toward total confiscation of all guns, long guns as well as pistols. And as long as the rural areas do not have high crime rates, then the people living there see no sense in taking any chance of losing their guns, which would mean the loss of a favorite rural pastime, hunting.

Of course, the confusions between "gun control" and "handgun control," plus the confusions between "control" and "confiscation," are perpetuated by the pistol lobby, in particular the National Rifle Association. By its unrelenting opposition to *any* form of handgun control legislation, whether federal, state, or local, the NRA has worked to sustain and reinforce the confusions of the citizenry, and to keep people divided on the question of handgun control.

There are several pro-pistol groups, but the National *Rifle* Association remains by far the strongest.

Just what is the NRA?

The National Rifle Association began life as an organization of Yankee Civil War veterans who were embarrassed that the recently vanquished Southerners had been better marksmen. Chartered in New York in 1871, it moved its headquarters to Washington in 1908, and has been there ever since. The purpose of the organization was to promote marksmanship, and the NRA has done that ever since through a variety of excellent programs that teach children and adults how to shoot guns—mostly rifles and shotguns—safely. My son Nick learned to shoot long guns at summer camp, and participated in the NRA's marksmanship and safety programs.

For most of its life, up until the 1960's, the NRA was content to remain what it had always been, a group of outdoorsmen who enjoyed hunting and shooting. They had a special deal with the government whereby they could buy surplus American military weapons at a discount. What's more, a member got a subscription to a fine magazine, *The American Rifleman*. In those days, the NRA was "fun," and many of my friends were members.

But then it changed. The beginning of the new, hardline NRA probably occurred in the early 1960's shortly after the assassination of President John F. Kennedy. Despite the killing of the President, and the cries for tougher gun laws that followed, nothing happened—because gun violence had yet to be seen as a *national* problem.

In the late 1960's, however, there was a tremendous increase in violence, marked by racial riots that were unprecedented in their size and intensity. And so began the rush to arms, which, tragically, took on the racial coloring of blacks against whites and whites against blacks.

After the murders of Dr. Martin Luther King and Senator Robert F. Kennedy, there was a public uproar and demand for congressional action. With pressure from President Lyndon Johnson, the 1968 Gun Control Act passed the House within a few weeks of Senator Kennedy's death and became law before the end of the year. For once, a highly controversial bill became law in an even-numbered year, an election year—but only because handgun violence had once again claimed a popular national figure. Congress dared not risk the voters' wrath.

And, for once, the National Rifle Association dared not stand in the way of the bill. In fact, the NRA came out in support, but only after it had weakened the bill with numerous amendments. Even then, the NRA's support was clearly condescending. A congressman, who was also a member of the NRA's board of directors, told his House colleagues on the floor of that chamber: "I think my colleagues in the House will be interested in knowing that I have discussed this matter with the National Rifle Association and with other organizations dedicated to the proper interests of law-abiding sportsmen and the reasoning I have advanced is concurred in by them . . . As a result, they interpose no objection under present circumstance to the adoption of this language by the House."

Since 1968, however, the NRA has become an aggressive, negative, and even obstructionist force in regard to any form of *handgun* control.

Mention the NRA to anyone today, ask them to identify it, and the great majority are likely to describe it as a *lobby* first and not as an organization of sportsmen. A great number of people would also respond that the NRA is a *negative* lobby, one opposed to progress. What's more, they'd be right. For, besides opposing any new form of handgun control, the NRA is now deeply involved in the effort to repeal our existing handgun control law, the 1968 Act.

Here is the way the NRA was described in a recent issue of the *Congressional Quarterly:*

MEMBERS: 1.85 million, paying $15 dues. Of these 290,000 are life members, who paid $300. Members include Ronald Reagan (since 1972) and 15 members of Congress, two of them—Rep. John D. Dingell, D-Mich., and John Ashbrook, R-Ohio—on NRA's board of directors.

BUDGET: $30 million, for a wide range of firearms-related projects, as well as legislative activity.

LOBBYING: NRA opposes all efforts to limit gun use, favors weakening of gun laws. Head lobbyist Neal Knox said NRA would support repeal of all gun laws, but feels that is not politically feasible. Five fulltime lobbyists, plus consultants Timmons and Co., Inc. represent NRA's lobbying branch, the Institute for Legislative Action. The institute has a staff of 55 and a budget of $4.1 million. It is backed by an extensive network of state and local gun clubs. Three hunting and shooting magazines, plus the Institute's "Report from Washington," carry legislative news and opinion.

CAMPAIGN ARM: The NRA Political Victory Fund reported spending $1.1 million in the 1979–80 campaign. About $445,000 was spent independently, with the largest amounts going to the presidential race—against Kennedy and Carter, and for Reagan. Another $473,000 was contributed to legislative campaigns. Campaign gifts went to liberals as well as conservatives, as long as they opposed gun controls.

LEGAL ARM: The Firearms Civil Rights Legal Defense Fund provides legal counsel to gun dealers and owners accused by the government of violating gun laws.

During the '70's, the NRA put on the coat of the single-issue lobbyist. In the 1970 elections, Maryland Senator Joseph Tydings was defeated when he ran for reelection. Senator Tydings had supported gun control and when he lost, the pistol lobby claimed credit. Political pundits offered numerous other reasons, among them that Tydings had been a special target of Vice President Spiro Agnew, and that a *Life* magazine article had hurt him with liberal voters.

Nonetheless, the pistol lobby claimed full credit. As a result, since then the phrase "Tydings syndrome" has been heard on Capitol Hill, which means that if you support *any* form of gun control, the NRA and other gun zealots may come after you.

Ironically, as recently as the '70's, the NRA continued to favor:

—Controlling the importation of all firearms and their component parts.

—Prohibiting possession of firearms by convicted felons, drug addicts, habitual drunkards, fugitives from justice, mental incompetents, and juvenile delinquents.
—Controlling all machine guns and destructive devices.
—Requiring licensing of manufacturers, importers, dealers and pawnbrokers, and their keeping of records.

Regarding a waiting period, the NRA stated: "A waiting period could help in reducing crimes of passion and in preventing people with criminal records or dangerous mental illness from acquiring guns."

This did not sound like an extremist position to them then. In fact, there were rumblings in the mid-'70's that some NRA board members thought the group could and should take a more *positive* stance on the issue of handgun control and thereby reestablish their "sportsman's" image.

Not too surprisingly, this led to a split within the NRA leadership. Certain extremists left the NRA and set up another pro-gun lobby called the Citizens Committee for the Right to Keep and Bear Arms, which accused the NRA of getting soft on the gun issue and proclaimed itself the real champion of the gun owner. Using highly sophisticated and costly direct-mail techniques, they began to divert funds that would otherwise have gone into the NRA treasury. Other gun groups also were established to challenge the NRA's leadership.

The NRA saw their support (especially financial) and their reputation eroding. In response, the NRA for the first time set up purely political arms: The Institute for Legislative Action, and the Political Victory Fund for election involvement. They also began to criticize other gun groups who were fighting for the same gun dollars. In one editorial they stated:

> Nearly a dozen organizations or fund-raising corporations have been out collecting money nationally for their proclaimed purpose of opposing anti-gun legislation. The defense of gun ownership may yet come to a grinding halt, or worse, for that very reason. The strength of those upholding the right to bear arms, once solidly marshalled behind the NRA, is now divided in the face of the enemy.
>
> . . . Every dollar sent elsewhere to other pro-gun organizations,

no matter how good the organizations or their intentions may be, divides the financial forces of gun ownership in the face of growing opposition to firearms.

That this can seriously weaken the increasingly strong stand taken by the NRA in the legislative field is now obvious.

In early 1977, some old-guard members urged the NRA to move out of Washington and reestablish itself out west. Colorado was the favored site. Some cited the high crime rate in Washington as the reason for the move, while others mentioned the need to become better identified (*re*-identified?) as an organization of sportsmen.

The proposal resulted in increasing bickering between the hard-liners, who felt the NRA's chief responsibility was to fight gun legislation, and the old guard, who wanted the NRA to return to early, less-acrimonious days.

Only those life members who actually attend the annual convention are allowed to vote—which works out to roughly a thousand of the 1.8 million members. It is not hard to see how a strong, yet tiny faction could actually control the organization.

Indeed, that's exactly what happened in 1977 when a group of hard-line members took over, ousting the old-guard group. Since 1977, the organization has been rabidly anti-control. As the *Washington Star* put it, in its recent series: "The old leaders, accused of being a bunch of environmentalists and bird-watchers who had become soft on pistol control, learned that the issue could be as hazardous for them as it could for the members of Congress on the NRA's political hit list."

Regarding the strange election setup, the *Star* quoted an officer of the California Rifle and Pistol Association who was ousted in the 1977 purge, on the point that the largest number of members ever to show up at a convention was 1,248 in 1980—which represented less than half of one percent of the eligible voters. "The way they've set it up," said Michael Opsitnik, "they can take over a $50-million organization with 625 votes. The Federation says this is election by the members. We say . . . if they call this election by the members, they must have studied politics in Russia."

One of the saddest results of the NRA's strident campaign against handgun controls is that the organization could be a natural proponent or *champion* of responsible handgun controls. Given the nature and the widespread membership of the NRA, plus its line of publications and newsletters, it has an almost unique opportunity for good: it could promote responsible laws that would help to keep pistols out of the hands of the criminal or the insane, while at the same time allowing the use of rifles and handguns by law-abiding citizens for the proper purposes of sport and —on a carefully trained basis—self-protection.

Even the nation's largest handgun manufacturer, Smith & Wesson, is for handgun licensing. According to David Wallace, chairman and chief executive officer of Bangor Punta, which owns Smith & Wesson:

> As the world's leading manufacturer of high quality firearms, the company has spoken out on this issue for the past ten years. Our position has been unswerving, and at a time when many ill-conceived and irrational viewpoints are being voiced, I feel our view is worth reiterating.
>
> First, the right of law-abiding citizens to purchase and possess firearms and use them for peaceful purposes and self-protection should not be abridged. Second, some means of keeping guns out of the hands of the mentally unbalanced, the alcohol- or drug-affected, or criminally disposed people must be found. *We continue to believe that a federal gun owners licensing law, together with mandatory sentencing of people who use firearms in committing a crime, would give the best answer.* (Our italics.)

The NRA could join with them in this approach. Instead, it has chosen an entirely different role.

Anyone who chooses to fight the NRA quickly learns that the NRA's favorite tactic is a conscious use of exaggeration and obfuscation. Playing on the fear of many that the government will not only take away its guns one day, but will also use lists of registered gun owners to find the guns and to control those good citizens in some unspecified manner, the NRA has been able to make even the word "registration" a flash point for its members.

Let's analyze their favorite slogans and bumper stickers:

"GUNS DON'T KILL, PEOPLE DO"

That's right—but only as far as it goes. People *do* kill people, in vast and increasing quantities, *but they do so mostly with hand-*

guns. And the handgun is a weapon that has no other function or purpose. It is designed and made for the purpose of killing human beings.

People also kill people with automobiles, and thus we regulate their use, but the many local, state, and national car clubs do not bombard Congress and the public with appeals for the un-regulated use of cars and trucks. Fireworks injure and maim, so we have laws controlling their sale and use. We ban open fires in dry forests. Parents keep poison, knives, and matches out of the reach of two-year-olds because of the high probability of injury or death.

Yet we continue to pour handguns into the homes and the streets of America with complete obliviousness to the increasingly deadly result.

In the cases of poisons and certain other drugs and medicines that can be fatal if used in the wrong way or by the wrong person, the government warns us by putting a symbol on the bottle or container. And each package of cigarettes sold in the United States carries a warning from the Surgeon General that they may be harmful to the smoker's health.

A few years ago, some legislators tried to do the same with handgun ammunition.

Senator Kennedy introduced an amendment in 1975 that would have allowed the Consumer Product Safety Commission (CPSC) to require the makers of ammunition to print on each box of bullets two warnings: "Do Not Store in a Warm Place," and "Keep Out of the Hands of Children." The pistol lobby rose up as if the future of the country was at stake, and the Senate defeated the proposed amendment by a vote of 75 to 11.

Not long ago, the CPSC came out with stringent regulations making gasoline-powered lawn mowers safer. The pistol people have no objection to safer lawn mowers.

"CONTROL CRIMINALS NOT GUNS"

That's a wonderful idea, but it shouldn't be presented as if the two concepts are mutually exclusive. Instead, let's try both. We have always, as a nation, tried to control criminals, and we need to continue to do so, by all means, at all levels—juvenile delinquency, law enforcement, judicial sentencing and parole, prison reform and rehabilitation.

I agree that we should put the criminal behind bars and let others know that swift and sure punishment will follow the use of a handgun in a crime. But while we are trying to do so, let's also make it more difficult for the criminal and the crazed to acquire their favorite tool, the deadly, concealable handgun.

Keep in mind a few facts: we catch only 20 percent of all criminal offenders; those we put away often come out of jail a far greater menace to society than when they went in; and almost one-half of all murders are acts of passion committed by the overemotional or the mentally ill, and are not committed in the process of another crime by criminals.

Let's change the slogan to read "Control Criminals *and* Handguns."

"WHEN GUNS ARE OUTLAWED, ONLY OUTLAWS WILL HAVE GUNS"

From the standpoint of raw propaganda, this is one of the pistol lobby's more popular and perhaps even effective slogans. It preys upon the fears of the law-abiding citizen that he will be defenseless against the criminal.

To begin with, the slogan is false because rifles and shotguns will not be affected by any handgun control legislation. Handguns, under any realistic set of controls, will still be available to responsible citizens.

All criminals who want guns can probably get handguns now, and they will continue to have them until we do something about their easy availability. Refusing to do so is part of the fight-violence-with-violence syndrome, which makes so little sense. If we follow that do-nothing path, by the year 2000 we will have 100 million handguns in private hands. When that happens, will we be —and feel—safer?

"GUN CONTROL WILL LEAVE CITIZENS DEFENSELESS"

Again, this simply isn't true. Citizens aren't noticeably safer when they have a handgun. Facts show clearly that a handgun kept for self-defense is far more dangerous to its owner and his family than it is to the criminal. There are far more accidents and acts of passion with one's own handgun than there are either criminal murders or preventions of criminal attack.

As police officers have said for years, the best defense against injury is to put up no defense—give them what they want, or run. This may not be "macho," but it can keep you alive.

Most crime utilizes surprise. That's why criminals prefer concealable handguns. And that's why most people who had a handgun on them at the time of an attack never got the chance to use it. The criminal and the crazed need that concealability; the homeowner doesn't.

"GUN LAWS DON'T WORK"

If they mean by this that the existing 20,000 state and local laws don't work very well, they are right. Without uniformity, the only way the crazy quilt of present laws could work is if we placed customs officers on every border of every city and state. This is one of the main reasons why Handgun Control, Inc. urges the passage of a *national* law to control handguns.

Or do the people who say this mean that *no* law will work? Would there be, in their opinion, fewer traffic accidents with fewer traffic laws, fewer burnings and maimings with no firecracker laws? Fewer drunks if there weren't so many liquor laws?

No law works perfectly, and handgun laws would be no exception. But does that mean we should never try? If one life were saved, wouldn't it be worthwhile?

"REGISTRATION IS THE FIRST STEP TOWARD CONFISCATION OF ALL GUNS"

Although this statement should be the easiest to recognize as ridiculous exaggeration, it is one of the hardest to dislodge because it is a classic example of the Big Scare tactic. This statement is a favorite of the extreme right wing, and part of their "Communist conspiracy" theme by which handgun control advocates are pictured as "dupes of the Commies who want to disarm America."

Such people have, I am afraid, very little faith in the American people and in American democracy. If I were afraid of a takeover, I'd worry more about the armed right-wing extremists than anyone else.

We should face the simple fact that licensing and registration are, or should be, duties of citizenship.

Licensing is nothing more than the law-abiding citizen standing up to his accountability. And registration is nothing more than that same law-abiding citizen standing up to his accountability for *a deadly commodity he has chosen to own;* it's the law-abiding citizen saying: "I'm a responsible citizen. Check me out. And when you find out I'm right, put the number of this gun down after my name, so that if it's ever misused, you know who to come and get."

That's responsible citizenship.

"AMERICANS HAVE A CONSTITUTIONAL RIGHT TO 'KEEP AND BEAR ARMS' "

"A well-regulated Militia, being necessary to the security of a free State, the right of the people to keep and bear Arms, shall not be infringed."

The headquarters of the National Rifle Association is a handsome $3.5-million, nine-story, stone and marble building about a mile from the White House. Above its entrance are chiseled the words of the Second Amendment. Well, that's not quite true. *Part* of the Amendment is presented there, the part about the right to keep and bear arms not being infringed. The other part, about the militia, is not there. The NRA has always been good at selective editing.

As I mentioned earlier, the interpretation of the Second Amendment promoted by the pistol lobby has never found favor with the Supreme Court. Five times the Court has treated questions of law related to the issue, and five times it has ruled that the "right to keep and bear Arms" is not an *individual* right, but a *collective* one that allows a state to raise a militia (today, the national guard).

As mentioned earlier, the American Bar Association, not known as a doctrinaire liberal group, reported on the subject (in 1975):

> There is probably less agreement, more misinformation, and less understanding of the right to keep and bear arms than on any other current controversial constitutional issue. . . . In addition to the five decisions in which the Supreme Court has construed the Amendment, every federal court decision involving the Amendment has given the Amendment a collective, militia interpretation and/or held that firearms-control laws enacted under a state's police power are constitutional. Thus arguments premised upon the federal Second Amendment, or the similar provisions in the 37 state constitutions, have never prevented regulation of firearms.

A little history may be helpful in showing that the Second Amendment has never had an "individual" meaning or intention.

Prior to the 1700's, there was no individual right to keep arms under the British common law. Nor was there a right to "bear" them. As early as 1328, there were gun regulations in England, and certain classes of people in the 1600's were barred by law from keeping guns.

In 1688, at the conclusion of eighty-five years of oppression under absolutist kings and military dictators whose rule was always enforced by a large standing army, the British Parliament passed the English Bill of Rights. This document, which reflects the traditional preference for a militia over an army (which was viewed as a tool of tyrants) had a strong influence on the Second Amendment of the United States.

Among the many things British that the American colonists adopted was the idea of the militia system and the fear of standing armies. It should be remembered that George III stationed huge numbers of troops in the colonies in order to enforce his oppressive acts, acts which led directly to the Revolutionary War.

Thus when it came time for the individual colonies to write their own constitutions and charters, most relied heavily on the examples of Virginia and Pennsylvania by including a preference for militias and a prohibition against standing armies. These documents, in turn, had an influence on the Constitution of the United States in the form of the Second Amendment. But it is clear that the right to keep and bear arms which all these documents mentioned was for the purpose of arming the militia, not the private citizen as an individual.

Several recent question-and-answer sessions with gun sympathizers repeat the misconceptions described above.

The first came in President Reagan's first press conference after having been shot. He was asked if, as a result of having almost become a statistic in the Handgun Body Count, he had changed his position and would now support gun control legislation. No, he said, such laws are not the way to stop the kind of shooting that almost took his life. The President said that even though the District of Columbia has a very strict gun control law, it "didn't seem to prevent a fellow a few weeks ago from carrying one down by the Hilton Hotel." He added that there are "20,000 such laws, federal, state, and local" and they are "virtually unenforceable."

What President Reagan failed to mention was that his would-be assassin, John Hinckley, Jr., did *not* buy his handgun in the District of Columbia, where the laws are strict. He bought it at Rocky's Pawn Shop, in Dallas, Texas.

One other comment made by Mr. Reagan was what actors call "a throw-away line." In answering a question at the press conference as to whether he would do things differently as a result of having been shot, he said that obviously security would be improved, then added, "I look back and wonder why it hasn't happened thirty times before."

That is exactly my point.

In 1975 Harlon Carter (installed in 1977 by the hard-liners as head of the National Rifle Association) testified before the House Judiciary Committee. Congressman George Danielson asked him: "So therefore you would rather allow those convicted felons, mentally deranged people, violently-addicted-to-narcotics people to have guns, rather than to have the screening process for the honest people like yourselves. Is that correct?"

Mr. Carter's response: "A price we pay for freedom."

Before leaving the topic of the pistol lobby, it is important that the reader understands their most recent—and to some, most frightening—activity. Everyone should realize that the NRA and similar groups are hard at work to repeal the laws already on the books.

A bill known as the McClure-Volkmer bill (originally called "The Gun Decontrol Act") was introduced in 1980 and again in 1981. The NRA has labeled it the first step toward repeal of the current gun laws.

To show congressmen and the public what the bill would mean if passed, we asked the Washington law firm of Wilmer, Cutler and Pickering to analyze its major features.

They summed up the consequences of the bill as follows:

 I. The bill would weaken existing controls on illegal transfers of firearms . . .
 II. The bill would interfere with state laws governing the transportation of firearms within state borders . . .
 III. The bill would reduce penalties for federal firearms-law violators . . .
 IV. The bill would make it easier for convicted felons and others to obtain firearms . . .
 V. The bill would weaken the enforcement of federal firearms controls . . . and
 VI. The bill is premised on a misunderstanding of the Constitution . . .

As a final note, here is what the *Washington Star* had to say about the bill in an editorial on June 16, 1981:

"REFORMING" FEDERAL GUN CONTROL

We have been reading through an interesting legal memorandum on the McClure-Volkmer "Firearms Reform Act," as its friends are so bold as to call it.

This legislation (Senate 1030, House 3300) is said to have some 190 co-sponsors. But how many of those who signed these bills have analyzed their aims and provisions? They would severely dilute the modest federal firearms-control law that Congress passed in 1968.

When the McClure bill was pending in the last Congress—that was, of course, before the shooting of President Reagan, his press secretary, a Washington policeman and a Secret Service agent with a "Saturday Night Special"—its sponsors seemed unenthusiastic about public hearings. They sought to attach it quietly as a rider to the omnibus federal criminal code bill, but failed.

It is disturbing that there is little appetite in Congress for a tougher federal gun statute, but perhaps understandable—so many of our federal legislators are cowed by the National Rifle Association.

But it is more than disturbing, it is shocking, that so many seem to want to roll the clock back to pre-1968 days, vitiating the pitiably mild controls already on the books.

McClure-Volkmer would do that in several ways. Handgun Control, Inc., who commissioned the legal memorandum cited above, is especially concerned that it will greatly increase the interstate handgun traffic (including illegal shipments) and undercut local and state efforts to contain it; that it would make the record-keeping that enables law-enforcement officials to trace firearms used in crime far more sporadic; and that it would curtail the inspections by the Treasury's Bureau of Alcohol, Tobacco and Firearms that help at least to keep gun dealers honest.

It would also make it easier for a convicted felon to obtain a gun legally. And it would weaken mandatory sentencing for crimes committed with guns where they are provided by present state law. These are only the salient provisions.

Now, the interesting question about the bill is this: Who would benefit? Who wants this dilution of the 1968 act and why? The legal memorandum that Handgun Control, Inc. is circulating on Capitol Hill shows how the bill's sly revisions of the law would work to undercut, confuse and weaken firearms enforcement. It does not tell us where the bodies—or perhaps one should say the treasures— are buried. There must be profit in this for somebody, possibly big profit. Otherwise, it is hard to imagine why people in their right minds would be disposed to vote, in effect, to increase a gun traffic that most of us find extremely menacing.

That is why public hearings are vital. Let those of us who think federal law should be headed in the opposite direction—toughened, not weakened—find out who is pushing this legislation and what's in it for them. "Honest sportsmen" and their pleasures, the National Rifle Association will probably contend, as usual. But we wonder.

It's slick business to call this a "reform" bill. The word reform, in politics, usually connotes advance toward a perceived public advantage. What is the public advantage in weakening the 1968 act? When judiciary committees of both houses begin looking into the bill, perhaps we shall find out. We suspect, however, that this "reform" is void of any such purpose, and that the only beneficiaries will be the pistol lobby and its congressional camp-followers.

9
"WE ARE
ALL VICTIMS"

"PETE, I don't know how you're going to respond to this, but before I show it to you I want to explain that it's a take-it-or-leave-it proposition. You can cancel it—and I can still put together another slide presentation in the seventy-two hours we have until the Eisenhower luncheon —or you can accept it. But you can't change it. Understand?"

I nodded. Charlie Orasin and I were sitting in the conference room of one of our consultants. We were about to view the first slide presentation that he and his staff had put together, a show we were to use three days later in Baltimore at a luncheon of fifty people invited by Dr. Milton Eisenhower. It was to be the first of a series of similar fund-raising lunches.

Someone dimmed the light, and I found myself beginning to perspire. I was afraid I knew why they had waited until the last minute to finish the slide show.

I listened to the narration, admiring the way the text and illustrations were integrated. Then, suddenly, I sat up straighter in my chair.

There, on the three-by-five-foot screen, in full color, was my favorite picture of Nick. It is a head-and-shoulders shot, almost in profile, and he is looking off into the distance, smiling. A shock of hair is blowing across and away from his forehead.

I think I began to smile slightly when suddenly the color photo snapped off and in its place—in stark black and white, and larger than I had ever seen it before—was the picture of Nick sprawled dead on the street in San Francisco. The same picture had appeared in the newspapers the morning after Nick was killed. And yet it was not the same picture, because everything but Nick's body had been cropped away, and the rest blown up to a huge size.

Nick was on his side, his face turned away, one arm twisted above his head, a leg bent. You could see one sneaker, the dark gym shorts, and light-colored sweatshirt. Part of his side and stomach were exposed. Slightly beyond him, on the sidewalk, lay a set of lacrosse pads.

"Oh, Lord," I said, and closed my eyes.

Today, that picture of Nick is used in our television film *The American Handgun War,* on a poster which contains the names of Americans reported killed in handgun violence during one year, and in a pamphlet.

No matter how many times I see it, I never know when the sight of that particular photograph will cause me to choke up. It's like telling people the story of Nick's death, as a way of explaining how I came to be involved in handgun control. I can tell the story twenty times in a row without a problem, and then for no reason, the twenty-first time, I break down.

Why do I go on with it?

In our daily lives, we're bombarded by statistics and after a while numbers become almost meaningless. I could tell you that 10,728 Americans were murdered by handguns in 1979 and you might be moved. But what if I took out 10,728 pictures of your fellow citizens? Say I used two versions: how they looked in life, and how they looked in death? Wouldn't you respond much more quickly and deeply? And what if, while you viewed a slide showing the dead body of a young man, you knew his father was in the room with you? Yes, you would be a little uncomfortable, and yes, you'd probably sneak a glance at him to see his response. But, *you would be moved.* That's why we used Nick's picture.

Our ability to move people is what will determine the outcome of the struggle that faces all of us. The starting point for ultimate success on the issue of handgun control is not the Congress, which —as the NRA has proved over and over again—will always be responsive to any single-issue group within its constituency. The starting point must be the development, nurturing, and expansion of a politically potent group favoring handgun controls in enough congressional constituencies to win on the floor of Congress.

People who are willing to vote for or against candidates on the basis of a single issue are people who are personally affected by that issue. People to whom the issue is only intellectual tend not to be dominated by it. As a result, on the issue of gun control, the anti-control side, being made up mostly of gun owners who are personally and emotionally affected by the issue, is more politically potent—even though in a minority—than the pro-control side which for the most part is not personally and emotionally affected. Clearly then, the political potency of the pro-control side would increase if its adherents were more personally and emotionally affected by the issue.

We came to see that in order to build a political constituency for handgun controls powerful enough to neutralize the NRA, we must begin with those who had been personally affected by the issue—the victims of handgun violence.

It is the emotional appeal of the victim's story which best assures communication, attention, and an *emotional involvement* on the part of those who are already known to be sympathetic on an intellectual level. Using victims is the most effective way, we believe, to conduct an educational campaign that will result in a constituency willing to vote on the basis of this issue.

Because handgun violence touches every segment of society, victims can be found everywhere. Thus, no matter what the political landscape of a particular congressional district, people can be found there who are just like their neighbors—except for the scars and anguish they bear as testimony to their status as victims of handgun violence. It is depressing but essential to remember that *anybody* can be shot.

As a handgun victim, I know how difficult it is to "go public" with one's tragedy. But I found that the more I spoke out, the greater the number of handgun victims who came forward to join us.

Our biggest break, in the sense of spreading word of our work, came in September 1977 when both *Parade* magazine and the television show *60 Minutes* did feature stories on Pete Shields and Handgun Control, Inc. (then still NCCH) and why he had become personally involved—my victim status.

Back in the spring, when I had been interviewed by the writer for *Parade* and the *60 Minutes* people, we did not know when either story would appear. As it turned out, the stories could not have appeared at a better time. The *Parade* article ran on September 18, and that evening's *60 Minutes* featured a twenty-minute segment on the NRA, which they ended by showing a shot of me. Then Morley Safer said something like "This man is fighting them, and next week we'll tell you about him and his group which is working toward handgun controls." The following week, a twenty-minute segment of *60 Minutes* was devoted to our work.

As a result of those two features, we were accorded what you might call "instant credibility." The phones rang more than ever, and the mail thundered in. The huge number of contributions and letters of support showed us that the polls were indeed correct in reporting that the American people favored some form of handgun control.

The response also reinforced our belief that the victims approach was the right one for us. Today, the "victims strategy" is part of every aspect of our work at Handgun Control, Inc.

We take very great care in our search for and recruiting of handgun victims. As Jeanne and I know so well, deciding to go public is not an easy matter. With some people we sense immediately that they cannot deal with their tragedy in a public fashion. And of course we respect that totally; we *never* push anyone to join us. In fact, only a small portion of our victims network is made up of people whom we contacted (from reading their names in the paper), as opposed to people who contacted us—became members first and then told us of their victims status.

In all of our mailings we now have a form which asks, "Have you, anyone in your family, or a friend ever been attacked or threatened with a handgun?" In the last year alone, over 10,000 people checked the "yes" box.

Jeanne sends a letter to those who answer yes, asking them to tell us how a handgun affected their lives—a handgun story, if you will. Then we follow up on several levels. Jeanne might give them a call, or they might get a personal letter from Linda Talbott, the head of the Victims Program—depending on the nature of their story, and their willingness to go public. Eventually we deliver these stories to members of Congress to show them what handgun violence is doing to their constituents.

What follows is a sampling of handgun victims who are working with Handgun Control, Inc. so that *you* won't be next.

ODILE STERN

On November 11, 1978, eighteen-year-old Michele Stern, a student at Emory University in Atlanta, was kidnapped and raped. When she tried to get away, she was shot to death with a handgun.

Not long after her death, a family friend of Dr. and Mrs. Richard Stern came to see me in Washington. He wanted to find out about Handgun Control, Inc. and carry the word back to the Sterns. When we learned that Dick and Odile Stern were interested in joining the Victims' Program but were still rather hesitant, Jeanne and I went to New York City to meet them and to tell them of our reaction to the death of our son Nick and how our work with Handgun Control, Inc. had helped us deal with the tragedy.

As a result of speaking firsthand with another set of victim parents, the Sterns decided to get involved. Today, Odile Stern is not only one of our most active victims, but a member of our board of directors.

In December 1978, Odile had written me: "You have done a lot of pioneering work . . . and we offer you our help in any way you see fit to fight for this cause . . . Michele's death must not be in vain. We also feel that because of her death, our own lives should, and will not be in vain."

As a first step, that year the Sterns decided that instead of giving Christmas gifts to their friends, they would donate the money they would have spent on them to Handgun Control, Inc. They also began a serious and time-consuming letter-writing campaign, urging *hundreds* of their friends to join our organization.

One of the things we always urge victims to do is to contact the media and tell their story, and the Sterns did this from the beginning. They also sent a letter to The *Atlanta Constitution,* in reaction to the conviction and life sentence of the man who killed Michele. In it they said, "We are grateful that justice was done . . . However, as far as we are concerned, Michele's case is not closed. We condemn a society which allows irresponsible citizens . . . to own .38-caliber handguns . . . Since November, we have become painfully aware of the epidemic of handgun violence . . . We have pledged our support to Handgun Control, Inc."

Since then the Sterns have held a memorial concert for their daughter at Fordham University. Odile made her first media appearance in May 1979, when she appeared with me on *AM—New York*, a television talk show. She followed this with many solo appearances on both TV and radio. Both the Sterns continue to support and work for Handgun Control, Inc. in myriad ways.

On January 31, 1980, Odile wrote to me, saying, "Just a year ago, we sent you a letter telling you that we had decided to support your group, offering you all the help we could muster. Working with you has been a comforting experience. Through 1980, graced by the memory of Michele, we will continue relentlessly to fight with you for our common goal."

And indeed they have. Odile Stern has been increasingly active, especially in helping *other* victims. Besides lobbying her representatives in Congress and working with the media, she has worked with a group in New York set up to help other parents whose children have been murdered.

All this from a mother who once wondered whether she could actually go public with her tragedy.

LOIS STALZER

Her son-in-law was murdered during a robbery.

On February 13, 1973, Mrs. Stalzer wrote her congressman, Thomas Ashley, a Democrat, the following letter:

> . . . I am writing this, first and foremost, for all of America, but
> primarily for my eight-year-old granddaughter, Tamy, and her baby
> brother, Steve Stone . . . After listening to my daughter sob all
> night over this useless slaughter, my granddaughter's conversation
> the next morning was as follows:
> TAMY: Grandma, why does God make bad men?
> GRANDMA: Tamy, God doesn't make them bad, they make
> themselves bad.
> TAMY: Well then, grandma, why can't the doctors make heads for

these people so they can get a new one and sell them instead of guns?

GRANDMA: *(No answer)*

TAMY: Grandma, when will mommy stop crying?

GRANDMA: Give her time, honey.

TAMY: Will daddy get dirty in the ground?

GRANDMA: Mommy told you that she got the best casket that she could get and that he won't get dirty.

TAMY: I could kill that man, and why can't they keep him in jail? I'm afraid, grandma.

GRANDMA: You must not talk like that, Tamy.

TAMY: O.K., grandma, but why do people have to have guns?

GRANDMA: *(No answer)*

Mrs. Stalzer ended the letter by asking her congressman to get the child's questions "to the correct department, and if anyone in Washington can answer Tamy's last question, we would certainly appreciate hearing from them before two more little children grow up in America with hatred in their hearts."

Congressman Ashley replied: "Seldom have I felt more helpless and inadequate. There simply is no rational explanation for the senseless and ghastly tragedy that struck your family and there certainly is no easy way of helping little Tamy understand why the father she loved and trusted is not with her . . ."

The rest of the letter was similarly sensitive, but the congressman made no mention of his position on gun control, other than to say that ". . . We seem to have a higher regard for the political clout of the National Rifle Association than we do for the elementary safety of our citizenry."

Seven years later Lois Stalzer, who by that time was working with Handgun Control, Inc., wrote Congressman Ashley again. Her letter ended with a question. "There are twenty-eight sponsors in the House of bill H.R. 5823—the Kennedy-Rodino bill—and I would like to ask why I did not see your name among them?"

One week later, Ashley responded:

In the past seven years, it's hard for me to remember a letter which touched and affected me more than yours did in which you related the conversation between Tamy and yourself after her father's tragic death.

And, frankly, I'm ashamed because in those seven years Congress has done nothing to curb the proliferation of handguns and thousands of other families have fallen victim to senseless handgun violence. The need for a rational and effective method to control handguns couldn't be more clear and I believe the Kennedy-Rodino handgun-control bill provides such an approach. I'm therefore pleased to tell you that on January 31, 1980, I contacted Chairman Rodino and asked that he sign me on as a cosponsor to H.R. 5823.

BARBARA LOGAN

In early 1978, we received a membership application and check from a young lady who enclosed a note stating that the previous fall, while a senior in college, she was out running at seven-thirty in the morning when a man in a car abducted her at gunpoint, attempted to rape her, and then shot her in the head. She was left partially paralyzed. She ended her note by saying: "Prior to my 'accident' I saw the need for gun control, but now I realize that everyone has to see that need, and I support your organization wholeheartedly and will contribute as much as I can—financially and *verbally.*"

We admired Barbara's spirit tremendously, and she was contacted immediately and asked to write a fuller account of what had happened to her. Not long afterward, she replied:

> I try not to think of October 14 as a date to be remembered but somehow, I fail. It was on that date in 1977 that I was shot in the head.
>
> No, the incident did not happen late at night in the slums of some big city; I was abducted while jogging at 7:30 a.m. in a small college town. I was a secure college senior doing well academically and captain of the school's field hockey team. In one instant my assailant panicked, and all that and more was changed.
>
> Because I was shot on the right side of the head originally, my whole left side was paralyzed. Where formerly I had been proud of my physical prowess and coordination, I was now ashamed of my wheelchair and of having one arm that looked "funny." I was in a hospital for three months and had to withdraw from school for a year. During the first recuperative months, my mind was in neural shock and the slowed thinking process was scary and frustrating. I despised being so dependent.

My self-confidence plummeted as my fears grew. Who would like such a physically defective person? Would I regain my intellectual abilities and stamina to be able to finish school? Would I ever be able to tie my shoes by myself again?

Fortunately, all questions were answered favorably. Today I have my B.S. degree, am living independently in a new area, and am very happy.

There are differences, however, which I would not have anticipated.

I walk with a slight limp. Instead of running for exercise, I swim. I enjoy tennis from a spectator's point of view as opposed to a participant's. My impaired vision makes it easier to rely on public transportation instead of coping with a car, and I've learned to turn my head slightly to avoid bumping into things.

My fingers no longer fly over a piano and I will never be hired for ability as a typist. Taking medicine is routine now, and when I start to lose my balance a lot, it's a sign I need more rest . . .

Although I don't like to say I was lucky (I was *un*lucky the whole incident occurred) I was *very* fortunate; fortunate my parents could afford medical treatment, fortunate I had friends to encourage me, fortunate to have regained most of my abilities, fortunate I lived.

I don't want others to pity me or to feel I've turned bitter. My purpose in exposing my attack and its effects is in the hopes that similar experiences can be prevented. My story ends happily; most do not.

I hope by expressing the pain I've felt because of a handgun, the irresponsible proliferation of these weapons within our society can be stopped.

Sincerely,
Barbara Logan

Barbara sent copies of her story to the local newspapers and radio and television stations. After one television debate where she had to face the "other side," she wrote:

Although at first it seemed that everyone was wearing an NRA belt buckle . . . I think the pro-control people definitely held their own and then some. I stated that I was a victim, and I think it gave me some credibility with some of those people. Sad that that's what it takes, but I guess that's why victims can be so useful.

There are various ways of getting involved in the Victims Program. Here are two examples of people whose initial efforts were directed at helping us raise funds. In the first case, Handgun Control, Inc. took over the necessary mailing, bookkeeping, and even sent the "thank yous."

CHARLES TICHO

Mr. Ticho is a slightly different kind of victim. He himself was neither shot nor attacked. But his brother was. His brother Steven was shot and killed, as he slept, by a burglar. Mr. Ticho is a survivor, and very much a victim too.

Charlie sent a letter to his friends and relatives asking for funds for Handgun Control, Inc. in order to form an ongoing memorial to the memory of his brother, Steve. Their contributions were more than generous.

ELLIOTT JONES

Dr. Michael Halberstam's widow, Elliott Jones, set up the Halberstam Handgun Control Memorial. Each month, the funds help pay for the publication of the "Handgun Body Count," which is sent to editorial writers and columnists. One such recipient was Ann Landers. She wrote:

> Dear Readers: Every time I print something about gun control, I am bombarded with angry mail promoted by the National Rifle Association. But here I go again. Maybe, just maybe, I can save a few lives.
>
> The National Rifle Association is a highly sophisticated organization with one of the strongest and richest lobbies in Washington. But they need new phrases. I am bored with "Guns don't kill people . . . people kill people." (We know people kill people. Who else? Monkeys?)
>
> Thousands of people who are now dead would be alive today if some hothead hadn't had access to a gun. Nearly 70 percent of this country's gun victims are shot, not by burglars, but by people they know—relatives, neighbors, friends. Often the shooting is

unplanned. If that person had no gun, he would have used his fist or a baseball bat.

Hunters, please note: I am not trying to spoil your sport. Rifles are O.K. It's those handguns, the little Saturday Night Specials, that ought to be outlawed by federal legislation.

I would like to share with you something received in the mail from "the other side"—Handgun Control, Inc., based in Washington, D.C.:

> During the Vietnam War, thousands of young people died in combat. Fathers and mothers throughout America lived in fear that their children might be listed among the victims. Although that war is over, their children are still not safe. Every day the American Handgun War kills somebody's son or daughter. Among those who died in the month of May:
>
> *Brooklyn, N.Y.:* Kelly Bowman, eleven, was shot in the head by a handgun wielded by two teenagers across the street. They were arguing about a record player.
>
> *Omaha, Neb.:* Patrick Rhodes, two, son of Mrs. Judy Rhodes, found a loaded pistol in the bedroom of his baby-sitter's mother. The toddler shot himself in the forehead and died a few hours later.
>
> *Cleveland, Ohio:* Mark Hintz, thirteen, was killed by a fourteen-year-old youth whom police have described as "a little John Dillinger." The accused murderer had made up a hit list with Hintz's name already crossed out.
>
> *Houston, Tex.:* Gregory Dupree, thirteen, son of McKinney Dupree, was killed in a vacant lot when three youths found a handgun and fired it.
>
> *Grand Coulee, Wash.:* Teresa Ybette, fifteen, was killed as she slipped on some rocks while carrying a loaded .22-caliber revolver. She had been given the pistol by two companions who instructed her to fire it in the air if she needed anything.
>
> *Queens, N.Y.:* Stephen Zwickert, sixteen, son of Mr. and Mrs. Edward Zwickert, was murdered near his home in an attempted robbery as he returned home from a prom. It was the first night he had been permitted to stay out so late.

> There are thousands more, but I think by now you have the idea.

The following victim has been with this organization since almost the beginning.

LOIS HESS

Like Jeanne and me, Lois and her husband Dick lost a grown son.

Today Lois, a victim activist *par excellence*, is a member of the board of directors of Handgun Control, Inc. It would be hard to imagine Handgun Control, Inc. without her.

Her son Stuart was twenty-four years old. Bright and very hard-working, he had recently received a master's degree in land use and urban planning, and was working for his father's building firm. He was a particularly well-liked young man without an enemy in the world.

Early one winter morning in 1974, he went to one of his father's townhouse development sites to check on progress. Noting a broken window in one of the units, he went inside to investigate. He encountered a burglar who shot him to death.

"The cold, inexplicable shock of his young life being wasted," wrote Lois on behalf of Handgun Control, Inc., "brought to mind something I had once read: 'When your parent dies you have lost your past. When your child dies you have lost your future.' As a mother, I felt the crushing loss of 'my future.' But I also vowed to devote as much of my energies as possible to fighting to see that other American mothers, wives, and sisters could be spared my grief."

As an indication of how hard Lois Hess has worked, here is a brief review of her activities on behalf of handgun control from the days following the shooting of John Lennon in December 1980 until the middle of January 1981:

Tues. Dec. 9—Channel 2 (CBS) News came to my house.

Sun. Dec. 14—Channel 13 TV: one-hour live talk show called *Sunday Live.*

Fri. Dec. 19—Channel 13: 6:00 p.m. news.

Sun. Dec. 21—WBSB radio: half-hour taped talk show.

Fri. Jan. 9—WPTX, WMDM radio: talk show. (Hooked me up at home with this call-in show and NRA person.)

Mon. Jan. 12—Showed American Handgun War film at Stuart's high school—eight times. Invited by Stuart's social studies teacher.

Tues. Jan. 13—Went to coroner's office and copied the
enclosed names. Also spoke at the University of Maryland
to social workers and medical students concerning what
one does when one buries a child.

Sun. Jan. 18—Had a group come to my home to film a
documentary for Westinghouse (Channel 13). Theme: It
Can Happen to Anyone.

Lois' note failed to mention that during that time she was also
coming down to Washington one day each week, as she always
does, to work as a volunteer at the headquarters of Handgun
Control, Inc.

Here is a final account that is an excellent example of how
movingly some victims are able to tell their stories through the
media. The second is the response of a frightened second-grader,
whose name we have withheld.

PEGGY ANDERSON

This is part of the article Ms. Anderson wrote for the *Philadelphia Inquirer:*

A few hours after President Reagan was shot on March 30, I called
my mother in Chicago. I need to talk to my mother after
prominent Americans get shot with handguns. I think she needs to
talk to me. When ordinary citizens are shot with handguns, we are
not usually required to confront our memories. Handgun killings
rarely qualify as news in America now. They are too commonplace.
Eleven thousand citizens were murdered by handguns last year. To
most of that carnage, only families and friends paid any attention.
But when a prominent American is maimed or murdered, the news
seizes the nation. Life stops while swarms of ugly details take over
the atmosphere.

And always, over and over, the details force into my mind the
picture of my father lying on the floor of his office with a bullet
hole through his white shirt, blood spurting in the air from a main
artery, his pupils fixed and dilated.

I've never asked my mother or sister or brother what images
push into their thoughts whenever there's a newsworthy shooting in

our land. I know only that we are bound by every one of these awful events to relive the most terrible days of our lives. When this happens, we need to comfort and be comforted. Nearly eleven years have passed since dad was murdered. The shootings go on and on. For us, they get harder to take, not easier.

My mother's voice on March 30 was almost no voice at all. "How many more times? I'm just destroyed. How many more times?"

10
A PROGRAM TO REDUCE HANDGUN VIOLENCE

I'M sure many of us share the ideal of a society without handguns, indeed one without the *need* for handguns. That is particularly true of those of us who have become victims, people who have suffered the ultimate loss of a loved one. Yet despite this ordeal, what I have learned about the issue since 1974, along with the basic values I brought to the debate, have caused me to guide Handgun Control, Inc. to a centrist position.

This is the most difficult position because it satisfies the ideals of neither side. Yet if we continue to allow the debate to proceed along purely idealistic, i.e., extreme, lines, I don't believe we will ever achieve effective handgun control nationally.

What's more, I think that's why the pistol lobby encourages this all-or-nothing kind of debate. They agree with me that such debates only serve to polarize the issue and end up turning off and even alienating the public. Consequently they achieve exactly what the pistol lobby wants—nothing.

But there is a more basic reason why we advocate the "control" rather than the "ban" position.

We understand the high level of fear in our society: fear of the criminal, the crazed, the drug-addicted, the violence-prone psychotic—fear that impels more and more Americans to buy handguns for self-defense. Don't bother telling them that a handgun in the home is more likely to harm a family member than to ward off an intruder. Such accidents and act-of-passion tragedies "always happen to the other guy." Arguments about the danger to children, the improbability of reaching the locked-up handgun in time, and the unlikelihood of outdrawing an armed assailant, will continue to fall on deaf ears as long as the level of crime and violence remains so ungodly high.

The polls have consistently shown that the people do not want an absolute ban on handguns. A total ban is perceived as taking away their right to self-defense, and until their fear is reduced they will never agree to such a law. What they do want, however, is a set of strict laws to control the easy access to handguns by the criminal and the violence-prone—*as long as those controls don't jeopardize the perceived right of law-abiding citizens to buy and own handguns for self-defense.*

THE KENNEDY-RODINO HANDGUN CRIME CONTROL ACT

When it became apparent in 1978 that President Carter was not going to introduce his legislation, we encouraged Senator Kennedy and Congressman Rodino to take the initiative. At the same time we encouraged them to take the centrist position we had been espousing and, in fact, with the help of our law firm, Wilmer, Cutler and Pickering, we suggested legislation reflecting that position. Besides these centrist philosophies, our suggested legislation was based on the results of the polls—i.e., what the public wanted—and the draft of the now defunct Carter bill. We purposely suggested very comprehensive legislation because we wanted to promote a full and open discussion of the whole range of options and possible solutions. We did not want hearings on the bill to focus too soon on only one small aspect of such a complex problem. We felt the public should be allowed to see how their legislators feel and vote on the full range of alternatives represented by the polls.

We worked closely with the Capitol Hill aides of both leaders and their respective Judiciary Committees. Although the resulting Kennedy-Rodino Handgun Crime Control Act does not include all our suggestions, it strongly reflects our centrist position, our desire for a broad, comprehensive approach and, I must say, a good measure of my personal philosophy about the roles and responsibilities of government, business, and the individual citizen in such a complex social issue.

In the following discussion of the key features of the Kennedy-Rodino bill, the concepts of *responsibility* and *accountability* are interwoven throughout. I firmly believe that those concepts are at the heart of our democratic form of government. Our individual freedoms are based on the willingness of each one of us to be responsible and accountable for his or her own actions, and the fact that some are irresponsible does not relieve the rest of us from that obligation. Not if we want democracy to work.

The pistol lobby says "control criminals, not guns." We say control criminals *and* their easy access to their favorite weapon, the easily concealable handgun. This is the focus of the Kennedy-Rodino Handgun Crime Control Act. However, this is not based on any naive hope that criminals will obey such laws. Rather, it is based on the willingness of the rest of us to be responsible and accountable citizens, and the knowledge that to the degree we are, we make it more difficult for the criminal to get a handgun.

Here are the key provisions of the Kennedy-Rodino bill, along with Handgun Control, Inc.'s reasons why we think they will help reduce crime:

1. *Stop the Manufacture and Sale of Saturday Night Specials*
You'll recall that the 1968 Gun Control Act stopped the *importation* of non-sporting handguns. The Kennedy-Rodino bill would also stop the domestic manufacture, assembly, and sale of these same weapons.

If it was responsible (in 1968) for Congress, with the concurrence of our handgun industry and the pistol lobby, to stop the importation of this primary weapon of street crime, it is just as responsible to stop domestic production and sale of these handguns. The Kennedy-Rodino bill does not change their definition. It merely says that if these small, easily concealable, low-quality handguns are that great a menace to our society, then stop *all* of them, not just the foreign-made ones.

No one really knows how many Saturday Night Specials are now being made domestically because our manufacturers, assemblers, and importers are not required to report production by size and quality, only by caliber, but estimates run all the way from one-third to two-thirds of total sales. However, a good insight into the market for these guns is derived from a study by Dr. D. E. Burr of Florida Technological University. From large numbers of interviews with law-abiding handgun owners, and also with criminals now in prison for crimes involving handguns, he found that only 12 percent of the law-abiding citizens owned so-called Saturday Night Specials, while 68 percent of the guns used by the criminals were Saturday Night Specials.

Congress considered the Saturday Night Special the preferred weapon of crime in 1968. It obviously still is. Only now it is made or assembled domestically.

2. *Require a Waiting Period for a Law-Enforcement Check of Handgun Purchasers*

Current federal law prohibits certain persons such as criminals, drug addicts, mental defectives, etc. from owning or buying firearms. But the 1968 law requires no verification of whether or not a prospective purchaser is such a "prohibited person." The seller is merely required to ask the questions on the written form shown on page 149, and if the person answers correctly, we take his word for it and sell him the gun.

The Kennedy-Rodino bill modifies this naive practice by requiring that unless a person already has a state handgun license which would have required such verification, there's a twenty-one-day waiting period during which time a law-enforcement check is made. The class of prohibited persons is not changed at all. Rather, all Kennedy-Rodino requires is that citizens who wish to own such a deadly commodity, with its high potential for misuse, attest to their responsibility by getting a state license or by being checked out during a waiting period.

The Kennedy-Rodino bill makes this provision applicable to both regular sales by licensed, commercial dealers and to private sales between individuals. Under existing federal law, private transactions between non-dealers are virtually exempt from any

DEPARTMENT OF THE TREASURY—BUREAU OF ALCOHOL, TOBACCO AND FIREARMS **FIREARMS TRANSACTION RECORD** **PART I – INTRA-STATE OVER-THE-COUNTER**	TRANSFEROR'S TRANSACTION NO.

NOTE   Prepare in original only. All entries other than signatures must be typed or clearly printed in ink. All signatures on this form must be in ink.

SECTION A – MUST BE COMPLETED PERSONALLY BY TRANSFEREE (BUYER) *(See Notice and Instructions on reverse.)*

1. TRANSFEREE'S *(Buyer's)* NAME *(Last, First, Middle)* *(Mr., Mrs., Miss)*	2. HEIGHT	3. WEIGHT	4. RACE
5. RESIDENCE ADDRESS *(No., Street, City, State, Zip code)*	6. DATE OF BIRTH	7. PLACE OF BIRTH	

8. CERTIFICATION OF TRANSFEREE *(Buyer)*   An untruthful answer may subject you to criminal prosecution. Each question must be answered with a "yes" or a "no" inserted in the box at the right of the question:

a. Are you under indictment or information in any court for a crime punishable by imprisonment for a term exceeding one year?		d. Are you an unlawful user of, or addicted to, marijuana, or a depressant, stimulant, or narcotic drug?	
b. Have you been convicted in any court of a crime punishable by imprisonment for a term exceeding one year? (Note: The actual sentence given by the judge does not matter—a yes answer is necessary if the judge could have given a sentence of more than one year. Also, a "yes" answer is required if a conviction has been discharged, set aside, or dismissed pursuant to an expungement or rehabilitation statute.)		e. Have you ever been adjudicated mentally defective or have you ever been committed to a mental institution?	
		f. Have you been discharged from the Armed Forces under dishonorable conditions?	
		g. Are you an alien illegally in the United States?	
c. Are you a fugitive from justice?		h. Are you a person who, having been a citizen of the United States, has renounced his citizenship?	

I hereby certify that the answers to the above are true and correct. I understand that a person who answers any of the above questions in the affirmative is prohibited by Federal law from purchasing and/or possessing a firearm. I also understand that the making of any false oral or written statement or the exhibiting of any false or misrepresented identification with respect to this transaction is a crime punishable as a felony.

TRANSFEREE'S *(Buyer's)* SIGNATURE	DATE

SECTION B – TO BE COMPLETED BY TRANSFEROR (SELLER) *(See Notice and Instructions on reverse.)*

THE PERSON DESCRIBED IN SECTION A:	☐ IS KNOWN TO ME ☐ HAS IDENTIFIED HIMSELF TO ME IN THE FOLLOWING MANNER

9. TYPE OF IDENTIFICATION *(Driver's License, etc. Positive identification is required. A Social Security card is not considered positive identification.)*	10. NUMBER ON IDENTIFICATION

On the basis of: (1) the statements in Section A; (2) the verification of identity noted in Section B; and (3) the information in the current list of Published Ordinances, it is my belief that it is not unlawful for me to sell, deliver or otherwise dispose of the firearm described below to the person identified in Section A.

11. TYPE *(Pistol, Rifle, etc.)*	12. MODEL	13. CALIBER OR GAUGE	14. SERIAL NO.
15. MANUFACTURER *(and importer, if any)*			

16. TRADE/CORPORATE NAME AND ADDRESS OF TRANSFEROR *(Seller)* *(Hand stamp may be used.)*	17. FEDERAL FIREARMS LICENSE NO.

18. TRANSFEROR'S *(Seller's)* SIGNATURE	19. TRANSFEROR'S TITLE	20. TRANSACTION DATE

ATF F 4473 (5300.9) PART I (2-77) EDITION OF 3-76 MAY BE USED regulation. This is the case despite the fact that it is known (from Dr. Burr's Florida study) that approximately 50 percent of criminally-used handguns are acquired in just such private transactions. That study estimates that another 25 percent of the criminally-used handguns are acquired from regular licensed dealers, while the last 25 percent are stolen.

Access to handguns by criminals is made more difficult through the transfer provisions in this bill, but no law will be effective if it is not backed up by strict enforcement. The Kennedy-Rodino bill is. Its penalties for non-compliance include stiff fines and jail terms, and in the event an illegally transferred handgun is used by the recipient in a crime, the seller can become *civilly liable* for the consequences of that crime.

3. *Put Criminals Behind Bars*

As many of the states are now beginning to do, the Kennedy-Rodino bill would establish mandatory jail sentences for the possession of a handgun during the commission of a federal felony.

That's the way it ought to be. Use a life-threatening deadly weapon in a crime; go to jail! Under Kennedy-Rodino, two years is the minimum sentence for the first offense, and five years for the second.

4. *Improve and Extend the Handgun Record-Keeping System*

Under current law, records are required for each level within the commercial distribution channels down to and including the recording of the name of a gun's first purchaser. The existing system does not require the recording of subsequent transfers after the initial sale. Tracing of criminally-used handguns thus ends at the first sale, even though we know most criminally-used guns go through several owners. The Beretta that killed my son Nick went through at least six owners.

The Kennedy-Rodino bill would broaden and improve this system by requiring that *all* transfers during a handgun's life be recorded by the processing dealer and sent to that handgun's manufacturer or importer for inclusion in the ten-year "history file" for that particular handgun. Tracing of lost or criminally-used handguns would be simplified down to one phone call. Illicit trafficking would become quickly apparent. *And no central gov-*

ernment file, or the bureaucracy necessary to operate it, would be involved! Keeping track of handgun transfers would be the responsibility of the handgun industry, just as it should be for the makers of any deadly commodity. Just as it is for the auto industry, or any industry that needs a recall capability.

Such a system represents responsible accountability by the owner, and responsible participation in the control system by the manufacturers.

5. *Encourage States to Pass License-to-Carry Laws Enforced by Mandatory Penalties*

Massachusetts has such a law, the Bartley-Fox law. It requires a license to carry a handgun outside one's home or place of business. "Carrying" in public without such a license is punishable by a mandatory jail term. This law has saved lives in Massachusetts and has reduced the use of handguns in street crimes.

In too many states the illegal carrying of handguns is punished only by a slap-on-the-wrist. Thus criminals carry guns and don't fear getting caught. This is wrong. We must separate the law-abiding citizen, who will get a license, from the criminal who won't—and then punish unlicensed carrying severely. The Kennedy-Rodino bill encourages all states to use stiff mandatory penalties to limit the carrying of handguns to citizens who are known to be law-abiding and who have a license to do so.

New York and Connecticut have recently passed such laws.

6. *Make the Selling and Ownership of Handguns Serious Business*

Handgun manufacturers, and the industry as a whole, must recognize that they are licensed to do business in a dangerous commodity. Today's licensing fees are ridiculously low ($10 for a dealer!) and there are now over 150,000 dealers licensed to sell handguns. It is estimated that of this number only 30,000 are serious, conscientious businessmen. No wonder it's so easy for criminals to acquire handguns in this country.

The Kennedy-Rodino bill increases the license fees for all those doing business in handguns. It also requires that all commercial licensees take appropriate security precautions to prevent thefts of handguns, and requires that all thefts and losses be immediately reported to the law-enforcement community.

Because roughly 25 percent of criminally-used handguns are acquired by theft, this bill also requires *individual* owners to report any theft or loss. We think that is part of the definition of responsible and accountable ownership.

7. *Transfer Enforcement Responsibility to the Justice Department*

Because there is a tax on the sale of firearms, the enforcement responsibility for our federal gun laws now resides with the Treasury Department. This bill transfers that responsibility to our nation's law-enforcement arm, the Department of Justice.

For any law to work it must be properly enforced. With proper resources, the Department of Justice can crack down on illegal trafficking of handguns, while securing the rights of law-abiding handgun owners. Now, because of lax enforcement by Treasury, illicit handgun traffickers don't fear getting caught. This must change, and under the professional direction of the Justice Department it can.

The 96th Congress adjourned without taking action on the Kennedy-Rodino bill, but on April 9, 1981, it was reintroduced in the 97th Congress.

In his introductory remarks, Senator Kennedy deplored the handgun attack on President Reagan, and then asked the same question that plagues any American who looks at the issue with common sense:

> Before the latest flash of gunfire fades from our conscience into the darker pages of our history, we must ask of ourselves why we abide the continuing carnage of the gun and the bullet, the murderer and the assassin. This time, along with our fears and our tears and our shared feelings, must come a new sense of public purpose, a new national commitment to deal with a public question that has haunted us for nearly two decades—the question of handgun control.
>
> Today we launch a new effort in the Congress to end the arms race in our neighborhoods and streets that nearly took the President's life, and that each year takes the lives of 10,000 Americans and wounds and threatens 250,000 more.

President Reagan may be the latest and best known handgun casualty. But he is not the only victim. By this time tomorrow, twenty-nine more Americans will have died in handgun murders, and 700 more will have been assaulted in handgun crimes. Every day, the relentless toll climbs higher.

Inaction is inexcusable. It is time for Congress to stand up to the gun lobby and face up to its responsibility to deal with the epidemic of handgun violence that plagues the Nation.

This measure is narrowly and carefully drafted to achieve its goal. The reasonable steps I seek will in no way impair the legitimate rights of hunters and sportsmen, or prevent law-abiding citizens from acquiring guns for self-defense. I believe this legislation offers the best, and perhaps the only hope to end the arms race on our city streets and reduce the unacceptable rate of handgun crime that brings sudden death to thousands of innocent Americans every year.

In his remarks to his colleagues in the House, Representative Rodino was both eloquent and pragmatic.

The direct relationship between handgun availability and increased violent crime in America cannot be denied. Nor should it be ignored. I pledge all my efforts to work for sensible solutions to stop the handgun deaths, and I am urging my colleagues to join with me in this commitment . . .

Also, many states have enacted tough gun-control laws, but their effectiveness has been stymied by the ease with which handguns are transported from one state to another.

The only truly effective solution to curbing handgun crime is a national law that keeps Saturday Night Specials off the streets and provides a uniform standard of accountability across the Nation for the ownership, distribution, and transportation of handguns.

. . . I refuse to accept the notion that opposing sides on this issue cannot find a common ground on which to base a rational, effective, national handgun policy . . . Of course, I am not so naive as to believe that the policy I propose will work to perfection. But it will save lives. Of that I am certain . . .

It is time we stopped shouting slogans and counterslogans at one another . . . We must find a common ground to prevent our society from turning into a killing ground . . .

It is time we in Congress find a way to translate public sentiment into legislative action.

As a taxpayer, you must be wondering what enactment of the Kennedy-Rodino bill would cost. We have some monetary estimates, but let me suggest first that in terms of our most precious commodity, life, this bill would *save.* Taking no action would cost far more.

The cost in human lives and suffering is of course incalculable, but it is possible to measure the monetary cost of such things as hospital care, lost work time, law-enforcement and court costs, and the vast number of security precautions we take throughout our society. By almost any estimate the total has to be in the *billions* of dollars.

On the other hand, the monetary costs of the Kennedy-Rodino bill are modest, since no new bureaucracy would be created in Washington to implement the bill. Most of its features would be implemented at the state level and, in fact, one of them—the record-keeping function—would be delegated to the handgun industry itself. Also keep in mind that some 22 million dollars goes each year into the U.S. Treasury because of the 10 percent tax on firearms sales.

A study was conducted by Philip Cook of Duke University on the potential costs of this type of legislation. He wrote:

> A generous estimate for the annual average number of handgun purchases by private individuals in recent years is four million. An upper bound for the gross cost of implementing a nationwide screening requirement is $20 million per year (subject to adjustments for inflation). The actual cost of this requirement would be considerably less since multiple purchasers would not have to get a new license for each purchase. Furthermore, as noted above, twenty-one states already have a screening requirement, and could adapt to a federal requirement without much additional cost.
>
> The unit cost of a manufacturer-based registration procedure is about $.60. Manufacturers would be required to keep track of at most 9 million transactions per year (including transactions between dealers), at a total cost of about $5.4 million. Since manufacturers are currently required to keep track of 2 of the 9 million transactions, the net cost of the new registration system would be about $4.2 million (subject to adjustments for inflation).

To enforce the law properly, i.e., to hire the appropriate number of agents and launch special programs to combat illicit trafficking, will of course cost money, but not the hundreds of millions the pistol lobby always claims. Remember the swine flu scare? Congress immediately appropriated $100 million. And, as Dr. Michael Halberstam reminded us, millions are spent annually to combat diseases that take only one or two hundred lives a year. Millions more are set aside for federal disaster relief. What about the *handgun* epidemic, the *handgun* cancer, and the *handgun* disaster—which take over 20,000 lives a year?

The American people want handgun control, and I believe they are willing to assume its relatively modest cost. It is certainly far less—in all the many ways of measuring cost—than the cost of doing nothing.

Some may say that the bill doesn't go far enough. I'm a pragmatist and a realist. A national law must be fair and responsive to the needs of the law-abiding handgun owners in, say, rural Montana as well as in urban New York, and also to the majority of people who don't own handguns and don't want to. If the people in certain states and localities wish to go farther, they can. But the fact remains that we need a basic national law in order for state and local laws to work effectively.

There are many minor provisions of the Kennedy-Rodino bill which I haven't the space to cover. In addition, there are ideas I favor that aren't in the bill, but which I'd like to see someone offer as amendments. These are:

—We need better information on who are the criminals and the adjudicated mental defectives in our society. Our criminal records files are poor and need improving at both the state and federal levels. To improve them will take money and a firm commitment from our political leaders. So far they have not seen fit to build an effective national reporting system.

—The Kennedy-Rodino bill doesn't change the definition of persons prohibited from owning guns. I think it should be amended to exclude from handgun ownership anyone with a record of using potentially deadly violence against another person, even though such violence did not result in a conviction. The prohibited class should also include all persons convicted of an offense involving guns or circumventing our gun laws.

—The bill should require applicants to have had, or to get, qualified gun-safety training during the waiting period. Perhaps the NRA could run the program.

In light of the Kennedy-Rodino bill, the basic difference in the relative positions of Handgun Control, Inc. and those of the NRA is that the NRA believes in prevention *only* through punishment; we believe in prevention *and* punishment. They are not the same thing at all.

As much as I agree with the NRA that the violent criminal should be punished and punished severely, such punishment does nothing to prevent the crime in the first place. We need to combine *after-the-crime* punishment of the criminal with *before-the-crime* efforts to keep his preferred weapon, the handgun, out of his hands. These two approaches are not mutually exclusive. They both need doing.

In fact, we will work with the NRA on after-the-crime punishment of the criminal if they will work with us to find a before-the-crime means of keeping handguns out of the hands of the criminal and the crazed.

We also agree with the NRA that our "revolving door" criminal justice system allows too many violent criminals out on the street again too soon. Whether the cause for these inadequacies in the criminal justice system lies in too lenient judges, too busy prosecutors, or our laws governing sentencing, bail, and parole, I cannot say. But I am sure of one thing: If and when Nick's killer comes up for parole, I will be there testifying that he should stay behind bars for *life!*

To repeat: Where Handgun Control, Inc. and the NRA come into truly sharp conflict is on what to do *before* the crime occurs. Handgun Control firmly agrees with the many presidential commissions that have studied American violence, that if we are to reduce violent crime, we must do everything in our power to make access to handguns more difficult for the criminal and the crazed.

Why, for heaven's sake, don't we take all conceivable precautions when we turn over a potential murder machine to a stranger? The law-enforcement community wants them, the public wants them, and I suspect the majority of NRA members want them too.

But the leadership of the NRA does *not* seem to want any precautions! They seem to want complete hands-off, laissez-faire commerce in any and all guns. Indeed, as I mentioned earlier, they seem to favor letting felons, mental defectives, and drug addicts have handguns. According to NRA head Harlon Carter's testimony before Congress, "That is the price we pay for freedom."

Whose freedom? To do what? The criminal's freedom to threaten, rob and kill at gunpoint? Or the law-abiding citizen's freedom to live in a less violent and safer society?

The NRA contends that the waiting period required for police checks would be an onerous infringement on the freedoms of law-abiding citizens. This is almost ludicrous when one considers how often the average citizen is subjected to a credit verification when buying something with a credit card; only when the clerk has made sure your name is not on a list of known deadbeats will he or she approve your purchase. Does the NRA think this is an unfair infringement of the freedom of law-abiding citizens? Consider all the constraints on hunting (such as licenses, restricted time periods, bag limits, etc.) which the NRA does not oppose. I think the real reason the NRA opposes verification procedures is that they simply don't trust our law-enforcement community, our governments, or even the judgment of the American people. I wonder if they trust democracy itself.

It should be remembered that the NRA does not simply oppose the Kennedy-Rodino bill. It's working hard to *repeal* our existing gun-control laws. Neal Knox, the NRA's executive director, has called the 1968 Gun Control Act an "evil law," administered by "evil men."

Clearly, the gun zealots want absolutely no controls on any weapons by anyone in authority. They want to let Saturday Night Specials be sold freely, despite the fact they are the preferred weapon of the criminal.

They don't want anyone to be able to trace handguns used in violent crime, which could help police catch the criminal and return the handgun to the rightful owner. They don't think the owner of a handgun should be held responsible and accountable for the proper care and use of his or her deadly weapon. They seem to think *anyone* should be allowed to carry a handgun outside the home, not just responsible, law-abiding citizens.

I wonder if they think 10,000 handgun murders and a quarter of a million handgun assaults and injuries each year are an acceptable "norm" for America—such as 5 percent unemployment or 6 percent inflation.

I wonder how they react to the fact that murder is now the

leading cause of death among young black males who live in urban areas.

I can't understand why they believe that adding two million more uncontrolled, concealable handguns to our society each year will reduce this massive level of domestic violence—or make us a safer, freer people.

I don't believe it. The American people don't believe it. I don't think anyone but gun zealots believe it.

The American people consider it just plain common sense that we should do everything possible to keep such concealable murder machines out of the hands of those who would misuse them. And we must do so if we are ever to reduce American violence, if we are ever to reduce the fear that we, or one of ours, could be the next victim, the next casualty of America's Handgun War. As Jeanne Shields wrote in *Newsweek* a few years ago, "Some people can no longer absorb this kind of news [of handgun violence and death]. They have almost become immune to it, because there is so much violence. To others, it is too impersonal; it's always something that happens to somebody else—not to you. But anybody can be shot. We are all in a lottery, where the likelihood of your facing handgun violence grows every day."

Or are you going to wait, as Jeanne also wrote, "until the telephone rings in the middle of the night"?

EPILOGUE— HOW YOU CAN MAKE A DIFFERENCE

O N Tuesday, December 9, 1980, I awoke in a highly emotional state. Handgun Control, Inc.'s board was to meet that morning, and I had a great deal I wanted to say to the directors. Normally, I would make no formal statement, or if I did it would be a brief one, but for this meeting I had written several pages of notes so I would not forget anything. This morning was different, for it came after some of the worst days for me since Nick was killed.

On Saturday evening, December 6, Dr. Michael Halberstam had been murdered.

As I mentioned in an earlier chapter, I had known Michael for only a few weeks, but I had liked him immediately. At the dinner party where we'd met, he'd shown a quick and intelligent interest in the work of Handgun Control, Inc., and he had asked all the right questions. This is not rare—I frequently meet people who respond positively and well. They too promise to help. Michael, however, did more. He read the literature I gave him, became a member of Handgun Control, Inc. and then, a week or so later— without telling me, he wrote and aired two television editorials which supported the need for handgun control and spoke enthusiastically about Handgun Control, Inc. and me personally. I felt I had made a new friend, and I looked forward to a long association. Then he was killed. Murdered with a handgun.

159

Jeanne has pointed out that we victims never know when some *little* thing will trigger a wave of painful memories (in her case, seeing an old car like the one Nick used to drive has done it). The brutal death of Michael Halberstam did that and more. It was a profound shock.

On Monday night, I was asked to appear on the Cable News Network for a discussion program prompted by the Halberstam killing.

I went directly to the studio from Michael's funeral. Also on the program was an NRA representative. In the course of the discussion, which, unfortunately, soon turned into a debate, he absolutely infuriated me by suggesting that Michael had brought on his own death by advocating handgun control. In essence, the NRA representative was saying that Michael Halberstam had advertised that he didn't like guns, would not be armed, and thus *invited* the burglary. Indirectly he was blaming me for Michael's death.

The NRA man went on to suggest that if Michael had carried a handgun with him that night, he'd still be alive. I guess the idea was that as he unlocked his door with his right hand, he could have had the gun in his left and gotten the "drop" on anyone inside. I can't imagine Michael living that way. I can't imagine any civilized people living that way.

And then, late that same Monday night, December 9, we learned that John Lennon had been shot and killed. Murdered with a handgun.

The very emotional session the next morning soon changed from a board meeting to an open forum on the tragic events and their relation to the future of Handgun Control, Inc. Had we not been so caught up in our own emotions we might have anticipated some of what happened that morning—but we would never have predicted the magnitude of the response.

The calls from the media, which had started before the office even opened, continued without letup. Soon our meeting was a shambles. Directors and staff alike took turns doing interviews, and late that afternoon I flew to New York to do two television shows. It went on that way for weeks.

That, however, was just the media's reaction. The reaction that really surprised and inundated us was from the public. From December 9 through the month of February, we called on every volunteer we could fit into the office to help us handle the public outpouring of support. The phones were so busy we could hardly make outgoing calls; the mail swamped us; our reception room was constantly jammed with people coming in for information and guidance. "What can we do? How can we help?" That was the constant refrain. During those few weeks our membership increased by more than 25 percent.

And then came March 30, 1981.

We had been surprised by the tremendous public reaction to the murders of Dr. Halberstam and John Lennon. We weren't going to be surprised this time—we were going to act as the catalyst for a nationwide response. We took all available funds (the $200,000 which had come in as contributions after the Halberstam and Lennon murders) and placed the following ad in twenty-two of the largest circulation newspapers in the country.

WASHINGTON, D.C., MARCH 30, 1981 . . . President Reagan, his Press Secretary, a Secret Serviceman, and a D.C. Policeman were all shot by a lone assassin with a handgun.

THE DAY THE PRESIDENT WAS SHOT
WAS AN AVERAGE KIND OF DAY.

San Diego, March 30, 1981 . . . The handgun murder of four people was reported. They were killed while at target practice. Jessica was two years old.

Boston, March 30, 1981 . . . A fourteen year-old boy was shot by his friend with a handgun after they had watched the assassination attempt on TV.

Nashville, March 30, 1981 . . . Steve Bruce Martin was killed with a handgun.

Philadelphia, March 30, 1981 . . . Vernon Lassitor was killed with a handgun.

Chicago, March 30, 1981 . . . Antonio Jimenes was killed with a handgun.

New York City, March 30, 1981 . . . James Angus was killed with a handgun.

America, March 30, 1981 . . . If it was an average day over fifty Americans were killed with handguns. Over fifty.

At the bottom of the ad, we included a coupon which we urged the reader to mail to the U.S. Congress via Handgun Control, Inc. We would then have victims of handgun violence deliver the coupons to the Congress. The coupon read as follows:

To: The U.S. Congress:
You work for me. So I want you to know that I favor national control of handguns *now.* Enough is enough.
Please care. In the name of God, please care.

We were gambling on the fact that the American people cared enough to get involved. The response was immediate and overwhelming. It took several weeks for us to open the more than 250,000 responses.

Clearly, the American people do care.

If America had a tough *national* handgun control law my son Nick might be alive today. Senator Robert F. Kennedy might still be making America a better place to live. Dr. Halberstam would still be saving lives. And John Lennon might still be urging us to "Give Peace a Chance."

To me, the past seems to be repeating itself. Handgun violence is again skyrocketing. It is again a major issue with the public, our politicians, and the government. In fact, our new Attorney General William French Smith has set up yet another task force to study violent crime in America. On the same day he announced this decision, however, he rejected handgun control as a possible recommendation. He must have been unaware of the five prior presidential commissions whose recommendations for strict handgun control apparently remain unread on the bookshelves of the Justice Department.

Just a few weeks before he was shot, President Reagan sat down with the leaders of the pistol lobby, a group which had spent considerable sums on his behalf during the campaign and openly backed him. They asked for his help in curtailing the enforcement zeal of the BATF, and also in supporting the McClure-Volkmer bill, which was originally called the "Gun Decontrol Act."

Although word of this meeting never made the newspapers, it is rumored that the President gave the pistol lobby his full support. Certainly his budget director, David Stockman, did so when he recommended major budget and staff cuts for BATF.

A few weeks later, the President of the United States was severely wounded with a Saturday Night Special. While I prayed for his recovery, I also hoped the attempt on his life might cause him to rethink his misguided approach to the issue of uncontrolled handguns in America. That hope was shattered when the President, who had promised to speak to the annual convention of the NRA, sent an aide in his place. The aide said, "Ronald Reagan has asked me to be here, and I think that's quite significant." So do I.

The aide continued, "He said he would have liked to have said it personally, but he told me to tell you that he is a member of the NRA . . . I assure you on my word that Ronald Reagan fully understands the tough issues facing America's law-abiding gun owners and he will do something about it." He would, said the aide, support the McClure-Volkmer bill, the efforts to restrain the Bureau of Alcohol, Tobacco and Firearms, ". . . and anything else that would reduce the burden on the right of people to have and bear arms."

I noticed that no one said anything about the burden on the rest of American society represented by the uncontrolled handgun!

But the President had more to say on the subject of his support for the NRA. At his first press conference after he had recovered from the shooting, he was asked if he had changed his mind on handgun control (as a result of being shot). The President as noted earlier replied: "There are, today, more than 20,000 gun-control laws in effect—federal, state and local—in the United States. Indeed, some of the stiffest gun-control laws in the nation are right here in the district and they didn't seem to prevent a fellow, a few weeks ago, from carrying one down by the Hilton Hotel. In other words, they are virtually unenforceable. So I would like to see us directing our attention to what has caused us to have the crime that continues to increase as it has and is one of our major problems in the country today. And that's it."

He had mouthed the NRA line almost verbatim. However, like the NRA, the President failed to mention that the handgun which almost killed him had been purchased in Texas, a state with lax gun laws.

So here we stand:

—Handgun carnage continues unabated all around us.

—The pistol lobby is working to weaken even the loophole-ridden law we have now.

—The President jumps on the NRA's bandwagon even though he was almost assassinated.

—The Congress pays off its political debt to the pistol lobby by endorsing their bill in near record numbers.

The American people should be outraged. Your government is supposed to work for you. You pay their salaries. You elect them. But on this issue they aren't working for you, they are working for the pistol lobby.

How can this be? Simply put, it's political power. Or at least the perception of political power.

For over a century, the National Rifle Association and its allies have been unchallenged on Capitol Hill and at the ballot box. These gun zealots have had one hundred *years* to influence America without opposition and to amass a membership and treasury sufficient to counter any efforts to achieve responsible gun laws.

Every member of Congress knows the magic words of the NRA: "We have 1.8 million members." And when their lobbyist comes to visit, the legislator gets the point that a significant number of those 1.8 million may be in *his* district. We all know that once elected, our legislators spend much of their time working to get reelected. They know how they got elected in the first place—what groups backed them both at the polls and financially—and they know their margin of victory by heart.

If that margin was small, you can bet your bottom dollar their legislative activities in Washington will reflect not only that margin of victory but who made it possible. When the NRA boasts 1.8 million members, the legislator knows that in his district that *could* translate into thousands of ardent supporters or thousands of highly vocal detractors, depending on how he votes on the gun issue.

Despite its blustering, despite all the claims that its power has "knocked off" Congressman This or Senator That, the pistol lobby cannot show evidence, cannot *prove* that it really was the difference in any senatorial or congressional race. Nonetheless, there remains the perception on Capitol Hill that it *could* be the difference. So most legislators, regardless of their personal leanings, cave in to the pistol lobby's clout.

The NRA is expert at using both the carrot and the stick. If you stay on their "good" side and do what they ask, they'll shower you with all kinds of goodies: public endorsements in their campaign mailings; members volunteering as campaign workers; editorial praise in the local papers; or direct financial contributions to your campaign treasury. But if you get on their "bad" side, they'll do everything they can to stop you from getting reelected. They'll back your opponent to the hilt, and they have been known to overtly mislead the voters about your stand.

For example, Congressman Marty Russo (Dem.-Ill.) backed a moderate handgun-control bill in 1976. During the election campaign the NRA sent out a postcard filled with character assassination and gross distortions:

MARTY RUSSO DOESN'T TRUST YOU . . . WHY TRUST HIM?

Guns owned by law-abiding citizens terrify Rep. Marty Russo. He thinks guns in your home make you a potential murderer. He's even suggested that the honest firearms owners of America are "slaughterers."

Russo's solution to crime in America is to "remove the guns from American homes."

That's why he voted to choke off law-abiding citizens' access to rifles, shotguns and ammunition by driving out of business ¾'s of the nation's federally-licensed dealers . . .

Russo is bound to try again to condemn and punish decent citizens because *he* doesn't trust them. Doesn't that sound out of place in America?

If you disagree with Russo's belief that you are a "killer," let your vote speak for you . . .

I'm happy to say that Mr. Russo is still in the Congress. But no thanks to the National Rifle Association's Political Victory Fund, which paid for the mailing.

I've mentioned the NRA's dangerous legislation, the McClure-Volkmer bill. The National Rifle Association heralded it as the first step in *repealing* our nation's gun laws. In Appendix M, we list the current members of the U.S. Congress who cosponsored the bill in 1981. Pay special attention to the amount of financial contributions each received from the pistol lobby in 1980. If your senator or congressman is listed, ask yourself who he or she is working for in Washington—you or the pistol lobby? And then ask if your interest is served by a weakening of this country's existing gun laws?

If you support any form of handgun control, you should be one angry voter. You should be angry at the NRA, angry at the President and, above all, angry at your congressman and senators if they're representing the NRA instead of you.

But wait a minute. Are you sure your anger is directed at the right people? Are you sure your congressman and senators know how you feel on this issue? Have you written them? Talked to them? How often? How fervent have you been? Do they really know how much you care? If they don't, you should be angry with yourself. Because if that is the case, you have just confirmed the current political wisdom on this issue, which goes something like this:

> Yes, as a conscientious legislator, I read the polls and I know that the vast majority of Americans support handgun controls. And that's probably true in my district too. But I also know that the desire for stronger handgun laws is low enough on their priority lists that it *does not affect their vote on election day!* On the other hand, those who oppose any form of handgun control consider it the *number-one factor determining how they vote!*

Given this situation, the politicians respond—as you should expect—to the people who care enough to vote the issue.

It's as simple as that.

If you don't care enough to have the issue affect your choice of candidate, then why should the candidates pay attention to your views?

If you care about this issue, if you are *angry,* then you *must* understand the following facts of political life:

One, we can win. The public response in December 1980 and April 1981 proves we have the numbers.

Two, to do so we don't have to win the minds and hearts of the NRA. They are the minority. We are the majority.

Three, enough of us have to convince the Congress that we care enough to have it affect our votes. Our legislators must get the message that their political lives depend on us *more* than they depend on the NRA.

Handgun Control supporters are the majority and thus they have political power no one, not even the pistol lobby, can take away—*if* we care enough to use it.

Here's how Louis Harris put it in analyzing his 1979 survey on the issue:

It seems there are far more people in this country who would vote against a candidate who opposes gun control than there are who would vote against a candidate who favors such controls.

Overall, 23 percent of the entire adult population say they would vote against someone who is opposed to handgun control. By contrast, no more than 7 percent would vote against a candidate who favors such handgun registration. This means that those who oppose gun control are taking more than three times as much political risk by their stand than are those who favor gun control.

These results fly in the face of the prevailing wisdom in the halls of Congress and among members of most other legislative bodies in this country. The widespread belief is that the NRA is so powerful in getting its own members to vote against a candidate, that any legislator who favors gun control can be defeated in a close election . . .

The current evidence from this ABC News-Harris Survey calls into question a long-standing assumption made by many candidates for Congress: that the National Rifle Association is one of the most effective single-issue lobbies on Capitol Hill. And the NRA itself claims it can deliver its members' votes against proponents of gun control, whereas advocates of gun control simply cannot muster their following . . .

If Congress were to pass legislation controlling handguns, and those who voted for it were willing to make their vote a major issue in their campaigns, it is likely that the issue would help rather than hinder such candidates. Certainly, such proponents would be able to point to the determined efforts of the NRA and other anti-gun-control groups to unseat them over this issue. But if those favoring gun control were not prepared to make it one of the dominant issues in their campaigns, then the field would be left to the NRA, and the will of the majority could be thwarted once again.

So far, few politicians have been willing to test Mr. Harris' thesis. And until they see someone else prove it at the polls it is unlikely they will, *which means we have to.*

We have to prove that there are enough people who care enough about handgun control to unseat some politicians historically opposed to handgun control. We have to beat the pistol lobby at its own game.

This is why we say that handgun control is a political election issue before it is a legislative one. And why we set up the Handgun Control Political Action Committee.

In 1980 we raised $150,000 for political action and tried our wings in six congressional races. In each, the incumbent congressman was either a co-sponsor of the NRA's McClure-Volkmer bill or had received major pistol-lobby money—or both. In some we ran television campaigns, in others we conducted organizing campaigns. Sometimes we did both. One of the six we challenged was defeated; we heard from several sources that Congressman Bill Royer (Rep.-Calif.) cited our efforts as one of the reasons he lost. We did not succeed in defeating the other congressmen, all of whom benefited from the Reagan landslide, but we learned a lot and we made some real waves. Those congressmen now know we exist, and that there's a pro-handgun-control constituency in their district.

Our objective was, first, to educate the electorate as to their congressman's negative stand on handgun control, and then to raise the priority of this issue sufficiently among handgun-control supporters to have it affect their vote.

Again, we employed our victims strategy. Each television ad featured a victim telling his or her story, coupled with the message that the incumbent had voted against handgun control. One of our most effective ads was used in Illinois, against Republican Congressman Paul Findley from Springfield. The victim was Betty Bradley, whose grandson, Brian, had been murdered with a handgun. A picture of Brian was next to her as she sat in front of the television camera to tape the ad. Several times in a row, she read the following message flawlessly.

> If I'd done this before, maybe my grandson would be alive today.
>
> Brian didn't die in Vietnam. He was just seven and a half when he was killed with a pistol by a man who assaulted him and then took his own life.
>
> Since 1970, 192,000 Americans like Brian have been killed with handguns. Not in Vietnam—right here at home.
>
> Now the National Rifle Association wants to repeal the few laws we have to control pistols. And Congressman Findley agrees with them. I'm sure he's a nice man, but how else can we ever get Washington to care if we don't defeat the congressmen who don't seem to care?
>
> So I won't be voting for the National Rifle Association's congressman this year. I'll be voting for the Brians in our lives. It can't help my grandson. He's dead. But it's not too late for yours.

And then, without warning, when she read "It can't help my grandson. He's dead" for about the fourth time, she broke. That was the version we used. When the ad was televised, the viewer saw this intelligent, sensitive woman giving way to the honest emotion of sorrow. For the viewer, it was a visual lesson in how one handgun in the wrong hands can shatter a family.

At the close of the ad, the following words were shown: "If Findley wins, the Brians lose."

Even before the ad was on the air we received calls of complaint from Representative Findley's office. Why were we running such an ad? Well, we explained, Paul Findley had supported the gun lobby's bill, voted their way, and accepted their money. To us, the form of our opposition was both logical and fair. In all, we received three calls from his office—from his legislative assistant, his administrative assistant, and his campaign consultant. But we held fast and ran the ads.

Findley was not defeated, but his 56 percent of the vote was surprisingly less than his 70 percent victory two years earlier—when he did not have Ronald Reagan's coattails to ride on. The residual message of our television campaign was clear: We exist; and we'll be back.

After the campaign, Findley wrote to many of our political contributors (whose names are, by law, on file with the Federal Election Commission) urging them not to support such a political effort again. Our donors found his reaction quite rewarding. Some were so pleased they sent us more money.

In each district where our ads ran there were immediate efforts by the targeted congressmen to get them off the air. I had personal calls at home urging me to pull the ads, lawyers tried to "persuade" TV stations not to air them, all sorts of intermediaries were sent to plead their case.

The most telling indication of our impact, however, didn't come until the next Congress. Many congressmen have shown a new respect for us, evidenced by the fact that they are now willing to listen to us. And some of them have even backed off from their prior co-sponsorship of the McClure-Volkmer bill. They know we will not go away.

We learned a lot in our first political-action effort, mainly the importance of meaningful numbers. And by numbers I don't mean just the overwhelming general support we have from the vast majority of Americans. As the political scenario I just described indicates, "meaningful numbers" means those who care enough to have this issue affect their vote.

These people come from those of you who are willing to speak out, who care enough to send in those coupons to Congress, who are angry enough at your congressman or angry enough at yourselves to sit down and tell your congressman that you want him to act on handgun control—or you'll find a new congressman who will. And if a congressman is unseated by his constituents because of his opposition to handgun control, the message will ring loud and clear to every member of Congress.

We had 50,000 such numbers in November 1980, and when you spread them over 435 congressional districts that's not many in each. However, today we have almost 500,000 members and supporters signed up *and willing to demand action* from their representatives. That's still not enough for the next political battles. We need and we are going to have at least *one million* active supporters on our team by the 1982 elections.

That's not an exaggeration. It will happen—because the vast majority of Americans want handgun control; because there are enough of you out there who are already victims of handgun violence; because hundreds of thousands of you live in fear of being the next victim; because for *every hour* we wait, one more victim will join Robert Kennedy, Michael Halberstam, John Lennon; will join Stuart, Michele, Brian, and our Nick.

And if one million people aren't enough in 1982, then we will expand our efforts, and in 1984 we will return with *ten million!* We know how to do it now.

There is a new political force in the land, and it is not the NRA.

It is you, and you, and you, and you. *You* can make a difference. *Together* we can win.

> HANDGUN CONTROL, INC.
> 810 18th Street, N.W.
> Washington, D.C. 20006
> (202) 638-4723

APPENDIXES

APPENDIX A

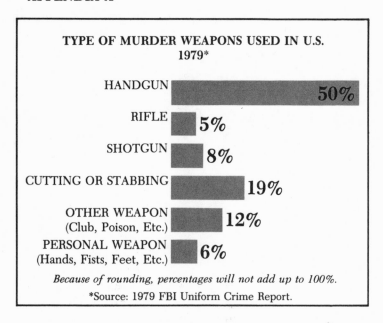

TYPE OF MURDER WEAPONS USED IN U.S.
1979*

HANDGUN **50%**

RIFLE **5%**

SHOTGUN **8%**

CUTTING OR STABBING **19%**

OTHER WEAPON
(Club, Poison, Etc.) **12%**

PERSONAL WEAPON
(Hands, Fists, Feet, Etc.) **6%**

Because of rounding, percentages will not add up to 100%.

*Source: 1979 FBI Uniform Crime Report.

APPENDIX B

MURDERS IN U.S. BY AGE GROUP
1979*

Age	All Weapons	Firearm
Total	20,591	13,040
Infant (under 1)	163	9
1 to 4	336	43
5 to 9	178	62
10 to 14	203	97
15 to 19	1,866	1,156
20 to 24	3,465	2,363
25 to 29	3,337	2,293
30 to 34	2,525	1,789
35 to 39	1,824	1,270
40 to 44	1,404	942
45 to 49	1,232	803
50 to 54	1,044	665
55 to 59	805	501
60 to 64	603	343
65 to 69	470	217
70 to 74	316	143
75 and over	443	134
Unknown	377	210

*Source: 1979 FBI Uniform Crime Report.

APPENDIX C

HANDGUN MURDERS IN U.S.
1969–1979*

1979	Total murders	21,456
	Total handgun murders	10,728
	50% involved handguns	
1978	Total murders	19,555
	Total handgun murders	9,582
	49% involved handguns	
1977	Total murders	19,120
	Total handgun murders	9,178
	48% involved handguns	
1976	Total murders	18,780
	Total handgun murders	9,202
	49% involved handguns	
1975	Total murders	20,510
	Total handgun murders	10,460
	51% involved handguns	
1974	Total murders	20,600
	Total handgun murders	11,124
	54% involved handguns	
1973	Total murders	19,510
	Total handgun murders	10,340
	53% involved handguns	
1972	Total murders	18,520
	Total handgun murders	10,000
	54% involved handguns	
1971	Total murders	17,630
	Total handgun murders	8,991
	51% involved handguns	
1970	Total murders	15,810
	Total handgun murders	8,221
	52% involved handguns	
1969	Total murders	14,590
	Total handgun murders	7,441
	51% involved handguns	

*Source: FBI Uniform Crime Reports for these respective years.

APPENDIX D

ACCIDENTAL DEATHS BY FIREARMS IN U.S.
1967–1979

1967—2,896
1968—2,394
1969—2,309
1970—2,406
1971—2,360
1972—2,442
1973—2,618
1974—2,513
1975—2,380
1976—2,059
1977—1,982
1978—1,800
1979—1,800

*Source: The National Safety Council, 444 North Michigan Avenue, Chicago, Ill. 60611.

APPENDIX E

SUICIDES BY FIREARMS IN U.S.
1968–1978*

1968—10,911
1969—11,304
1970—11,772
1971—12,288
1972—13,348
1973—13,317
1974—14,345
1975—14,873
1976—14,728
1977—16,084
1978—15,387

*Source: The National Center for Health Statistics, 3700 East-West Highway, Hyattsville, Md. 20782.

APPENDIX F

HANDGUNS PRODUCED IN U.S.
(excluding military)
1966–1980*

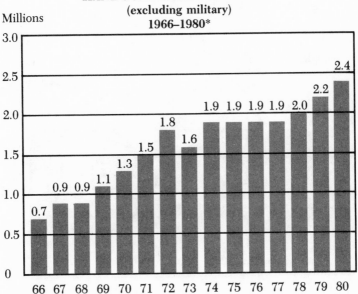

*Source:
U.S. Department of Treasury (Bureau of Alcohol, Tobacco and Firearms).

APPENDIX G

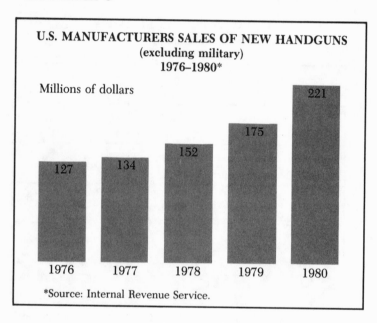

U.S. MANUFACTURERS SALES OF NEW HANDGUNS
(excluding military)
1976–1980*

Millions of dollars

127 134 152 175 221

1976 1977 1978 1979 1980

*Source: Internal Revenue Service.

APPENDIX H

PISTOLS AND REVOLVERS DISTRIBUTED WITHIN THE U. S.
(per thousand units and excluding military)
1960–1980*

Calendar Year	Production	Imports	Exports	Net Distributed
1960	475	128	85[e]	518
1961	447	115	85[e]	477
1962	431	168	85[e]	514
1963	453	233	85[e]	631
1964	491	253	85[e]	659
1965	666	347	87	926
1966	700	513	97	1116
1967	926[e]	747	96	1577
1968	900[e]	1155	92	1963
1969	1100[e]	349	87	1362
1970	1300[e]	227	179	1348
1971	1500[e]	346	132	1714
1972	1800[e]	293	152	1941
1973	1623	310	119	1814
1974	1895	326	133	2088
1975	1878	296	225	1949
1976	1891	175	249	1817
1977	1867	176	265	1775
1978	1957	191	255	1893
1979	2166	232	220	2178
1980	2371	216	193	2394

*Sources: PRODUCTION. 1960–1966—*Firearms and Violence in American Life.* 1967–1972—Estimated by Handgun Control, Inc. 1973–1980—Manufacturers' Reports to BATF. IMPORTS AND EXPORTS. U.S. Census Bureau (exports 1960–1964 estimated by Handgun Control, Inc.

*e = estimated

APPENDIX I

IMPORTS OF PISTOL AND REVOLVER PARTS BY CUSTOMS DISTRICT
(per thousand dollars' worth)
1976–1980*

Customs District	1976	1977	1978	1979	1980
Baltimore	67	48	21	43	80
Miami	1088	1869	2747	3825	3893
New York	368	525	760	705	700
St. Louis	146	140	243	134	169
Philadelphia	3	5	54	15	1
San Diego	34	3	—	—	—
San Francisco	30	18	25	13	12
Washington, D.C.	58	38	207	611	1087
All other	12	34	25	14	158
Total	1806	2680	4082	5360	6200

*Source: U.S. Census Bureau.

APPENDIX J

PRINCIPAL FOREIGN SOURCES OF HANDGUNS
IMPORTED INTO THE U. S.
1976–1980*

Source	1976	1977	1978	1979	1980
	Quantity (units)				
Belgium	13,225	12,079	13,053	11,512	24,635
Italy	28,018	53,823	52,905	62,123	64,233
West Germany	63,421	57,215	64,061	61,760	34,746
Brazil	33,929	19,749	37,084	57,621	66,968
Spain	31,781	31,019	17,097	30,445	19,396
Argentina	375	1,050	1,268	2,943	3,044
Hong Kong	0	0	0	0	2,961
U. Kingdom	82	6	41	1	146
All other	4,661	731	5,219	5,215	366
Total	175,492	175,672	190,728	231,620	216,495

*Source: Official statistics of the U.S. Department of Commerce.

181

NUMBER OF FEDERAL FIREARMS LICENSEES AS OF JANUARY 1, 1981*

Manufacturers, firearms	496
Manufacturers, destructive devices	44
Dealers in firearms, wholesale or retail	157,655
Dealers in destructive devices	7
Pawnbrokers	3,673
Collectors, dealers in antiques	5,541
Manufacturers, ammunition	8,997
Importers, firearms	444
Importers, destructive devices	13
Total	176,870

As federally licensed gun dealerships have risen . . .

(In thousands)

. . . the number of Treasury Inspections has fallen.

(In thousands)

Reagan cuts would reduce them even more.

*Source: U. S. Bureau of Alcohol, Tobacco, and Firearms.

182

APPENDIX L

CO-SPONSORS OF THE
KENNEDY-RODINO HANDGUN CRIME CONTROL BILL
S. 974 AND H.R. 3200
(as of August 1, 1981)

SENATE

Sen. John H. Chafee (R-R.I.)
Sen. Daniel K. Inouye (D-Hi.)
Sen. Edward M. Kennedy (D-Mass.)
Sen. Daniel P. Moynihan (D-N.Y.)
Sen. Spark M. Matsunaga (D-Hi.)
Sen. Claiborne Pell (D-R.I.)
Sen. Charles H. Percy (R-Ill.)
Sen. Paul E. Tsongas (D-Mass.)
Sen. Harrison A. Williams (D-N.J.)

HOUSE

Rep. Daniel K. Akaka (D-Hi.-2*)
Rep. Michael D. Barnes (D-Md.-8)
Rep. Anthony C. Beilenson (D-Calif.-23)
Rep. Jonathan B. Bingham (D-N.Y.-22)
Rep. David E. Bonior (D-Miss.-12)
Rep. George E. Brown, Jr. (D-Calif.-36)
Rep. Phillip Burton (D-Calif.-6)
Rep. Shirley A. Chisholm (D-N.Y.-12)
Rep. William C. Clay (D-Mo.-1)
Rep. Cardiss A. Collins (D-Ill.-7)
Del. Baltasar Corrada (D-P.R.)
Rep. William J. Coyne (D-Pa.-14)
Rep. Ronald V. Dellums (D-Calif.-8)
Del. Ron DeLugo (D-V.I.)
Rep. Julian C. Dixon (D-Calif.-28)
Rep. Brian Donnelly (D-Mass.-11)
Rep. Thomas J. Downey (D-N.Y.-2)
Rep. Bernard J. Dwyer (D-N.J.-15)
Rep. Robert W. Edgar (D-Pa.-7)
Rep. Don Edwards (D-Calif.-10)
Rep. John G. Gary (D-Ill.-5)
Rep. Dante B. Fascell (D-Fla.-15)
Del. Walter Fauntroy (D-D.C.)
Rep. Geraldine A. Ferraro (D-N.Y.-9)
Rep. Thomas M. Foglietta (D-Pa.-1)
Rep. Robert Garcia (D-N.Y.-21)
Rep. S. William Green (R-N.Y.-18)
Rep. Frank Guarini (D-N.J.-14)
Rep. Cecil L. Heftel (D-Hi.-1)
Rep. William Lehman (D-Fla.-13)
Rep. Mickey Leland (D-Tex.-18)
Rep. Edward J. Markey (D-Mass.-7)
Rep. Paul N. McCloskey (R-Calif.-12)
Rep. Stewart B. McKinney (R-Conn.-4)
Rep. Parren A. Mitchell (D-Md.-7)

SENATE

HOUSE

Rep. John J. Moakley (D-Mass.-9)
Rep. Toby A. Moffett (D-Conn.-6)
Rep. Richard L. Ottinger (D-N.Y.-24)
Rep. Jerry M. Patterson (D-Calif.-38)
Rep. Charles B. Rangel (D-N.Y.-19)
Rep. Frederick W. Richmond (D-N.Y.-14)
Rep. Peter W. Rodino (D-N.J.-10)
Rep. Benjamin S. Rosenthal (D-N.Y.-8)
Rep. James H. Scheuer (D-N.Y.-11)
Rep. Claudine Schneider (R-R.I.-2)
Rep. Charles E. Schumer (D-N.Y.-16)
Rep. John F. Seiberling (D-Oh.-14)
Rep. Stephen A. Solarz (D-N.Y.-13)
Rep. Fortney Stark (D-Calif.-9)
Rep. Louis Stokes (D-Oh.-21)
Rep. Gerry E. Studds (D-Mass.-12)
Rep. Henry A. Waxman (D-Calif.-24)
Rep. Ted S. Weiss (D-N.Y.-20)
Rep. Sidney R. Yates (D-Ill.-9)

*District number.

APPENDIX M

Friends of the Pistol Lobby in the U.S. Congress

This is a list of senators and congressmen who either received political contributions from the pro-gun lobby during the 1980 campaign, or are co-sponsors of the McClure-Volkmer bill, or both.

An asterick in front of a name indicates that the congressman or senator is a co-sponsor of the McClure-Volkmer bill as of August 1, 1981.

RECIPIENT OF SUPPORT	TOTAL	RECIPIENT OF SUPPORT	TOTAL
Alabama		**California**	
*Sen. Howell Heflin (D)		*Sen. S. I. Hayakawa (R)	
*Sen. Jeremiah Denton (R)	1,500	*Rep. Gene Chappie (R-1)	3,500
*Rep. Wm. Dickinson (R-2)	450	*Rep. Don Clausen (R-2)	2,300
*Rep. Bill Nichols (D-3)	700	*Rep. Norman Shumway (R-14)	750
*Rep. Tom Bevill (D-4)		*Rep. Chip Pashayan (R-17)	3,900
*Rep. Albert Smith (R-6)	1,250	Rep. William Thomas (R-18)	450
*Rep. Richard Shelby (D-7)	1,500	*Rep. Robert Lagomarsino (R-19)	
		*Rep. Barry Goldwater, Jr. (R-20)	
Alaska		Rep. Bobbi Fiedler (R-21)	12,100
*Sen. Ted Stevens (R)		Rep. Carlos Moorhead (R-22)	700
*Sen. Frank Murkowski (R)	1,000	*Rep. John Rousselot (R-26)	1,550
*Rep. Don Young (R)	2,975	*Rep. Robert Doman (R-27)	5,250
		Rep. Glenn Anderson (D-32)	100
Arizona		*Rep. Wayne Grisham (R-33)	1,464
*Sen. Dennis DeConcini (D)	750	Rep. Dan Lungren (R-34)	1,400
*Sen. Barry Goldwater (R)	7,150	*Rep. David Dreier	5,500
Rep. John Rhodes (R-1)	500	Rep. Jerry Lewis (R-37)	850
*Rep. Bob Stump (D-3)	550	*Rep. Wm. Dannemeyer (R-39)	100
*Rep. Eldon Rudd (R-4)	700	Rep. Robert Badham (R-40)	150
		Rep. Bill Lowery (R-41)	1,000
Arkansas		*Rep. Duncan Hunter (R-42)	3,000
*Rep. William J. Alexander (D-1)		Rep. Clair Burgener (R-43)	500
Rep. Ed Bethune (R-2)	500		
*Rep. J. P. Hammerschmidt (R-3)	250		
*Rep. Beryl Anthony (D-4)			

RECIPIENT OF SUPPORT	TOTAL
Colorado	
*Sen. William Armstrong (R)	
*Rep. Ray Kogovsek (D-3)	1,100
Rep. Hank Brown (R-4)	6,662
*Rep. Kenneth Kramer (R-5)	2,500
Connecticut	
Rep. Larry DeNardis (R-3)	1,000
Delaware	
Rep. Thomas Evans (R)	200
Florida	
*Sen. Lawton Chiles (D)	
*Sen. Paula Hawkins (R)	8,000
*Rep. Earl Hutto (D-1)	
*Rep. Don Fuqua (D-2)	100
*Rep. Wm. Chappell (D-4)	250
Rep. Wm. McCollum (R-5)	1,500
*Rep. Sam Gibbons (D-7)	
*Rep. Andy Ireland (D-8)	750
*Rep. L. A. Bafalis (R-10)	
Rep. Dan Mica (D-11)	125
*Rep. Clay Shaw (R-12)	8,127
Rep. Claude Pepper (D-14)	250
Georgia	
*Sen. Mack Mattingly (R)	1,250
*Rep. Ronald Ginn (D-1)	
*Rep. Newton Gingrich (R-6)	
*Rep. Larry McDonald (D-7)	1,700
*Sen. Billy Lee Evans (D-8)	
Rep. Ed Jenkins (D-9)	150
*Rep. Doug Barnard (D-10)	200
Idaho	
*Sen. James McClure (R)	
*Sen. Steve Symms (R)	13,000
*Rep. Larry Craig (R-1)	
*Rep. George Hansen (R-2)	600

RECIPIENT OF SUPPORT	TOTAL
Illinois	
*Rep. Philip M. Crane (R-12)	
*Rep. Tom Corcoran (R-15)	
Rep. George O'Brien (R-17)	300
Rep. Robert Michel (R-18)	200
Rep. Paul Findley (R-20)	5,246
*Rep. Daniel Crane (R-22)	3,903
Indiana	
*Sen. Dan Quayle (R)	1,000
Rep. Jack Hiler (R-3)	6,134
*Rep. Daniel Coats (R-4)	500
*Rep. Dave Evans (D-6)	500
Rep. Joel Deckard (R-8)	2,150
Rep. Lee Hamilton (D-9)	1,103
Iowa	
*Sen. Charles Grassley (R)	65,206
*Sen. Roger Jepsen (R)	3,350
*Rep. Cooper Evans (R-3)	1,262
Kansas	
Sen. Robert Dole (R)	1,750
Sen. Nancy Kassebaum (R)	150
*Rep. Pat Roberts (R-1)	750
*Rep. Jim Jeffries (R-2)	4,200
Rep. Larry Winn (R-3)	500
*Rep. Robert Whittaker (R-5)	325
Montana	
*Sen. Max Baucus (D)	
*Sen. John Melcher (D)	500
*Rep. Pat Williams (D-1)	
*Rep. Ron Marlenee (R-2)	500

RECIPIENT OF SUPPORT	TOTAL	RECIPIENT OF SUPPORT	TOTAL
Nebraska		**New York**	
*Sen. Edward Zorinsky (D)		*Sen. Alfonse D'Amato (R)	22,259
*Sen. J. James Exon (D)		*Rep. Wm. Carney (R-1)	14,006
Rep. Doug Bereuter (R-1)	1,547	Rep. Greg Carman (R-3)	5,549
*Rep. Harold Daub (R-2)	4,250	Rep. Norman Lent (R-4)	100
*Rep. Virginia Smith (R-3)	200	Rep. Raymond McGrath (R-5)	4,829
		*Rep. John LeBoutillier (R-6)	1,000
Nevada		Rep. Leo Zeferetti (D-15)	2,900
*Sen. Howard Cannon (D)		Rep. Guy Molinari (R-17)	6,847
*Sen. Paul Laxalt (R)	1,000	Rep. Hamilton Fish (R-25)	300
*Rep. James Santini (D)	1,300	*Rep. Benjamin Gilman (R-26)	
		*Rep. Matthew McHugh (D-27)	100
New Hampshire		*Rep. Gerald Solomon (R-29)	1,575
*Sen. Gordon Humphrey (R)	2,200	Rep. David Martin (R-30)	7,317
*Rep. Norman D'Amours (D-1)	1,500	*Rep. Donald Mitchell (R-31)	500
Rep. Judd Gregg (R-2)	500	Rep. George Wortley (R-32)	7,568
		Rep. Gary Lee (R-33)	937
New Jersey		Rep. Frank Horton (R-34)	37
Sen. Bill Bradley (D)	400	Rep. Barber Conable (R-35)	37
Rep. James Florio (D-1)	150	Rep. John LaFalce (D-36)	37
Rep. Christopher Smith (R-4)	500	Rep. Henry Nowak (D-27)	37
Rep. Edwin Forsythe (R-6)	200	Rep. Jack Kemp (R-38)	37
Rep. Harold Hollenbeck (R-9)	2,000	Rep. Stanley Lundine (D-39)	37
Rep. James Courter (R-13)	1,125		
New Mexico			
*Sen. Harrison Schmitt (R)			
*Sen. Pete Domenici (R)	250		
Rep. Manuel Lujan (R-1)	650		
Rep. Joe Skeen (R-2)	500		

RECIPIENT OF SUPPORT	TOTAL	RECIPIENT OF SUPPORT	TOTAL
North Carolina		**Massachusetts**	
*Sen. Jesse Helms (R)		Rep. Silvio Conte (R-1)	100
*Sen. John East (R)	4,500	Rep. Margaret Heckler (R-10)	150
*Rep. Walter Jones (D-1)	250		
*Rep. L.H. Fountain (D-2)		**Michigan**	
*Rep. Charles Whitley (D-3)		Rep. Harold Sawyer (R-5)	500
Rep. Ike Andrews (D-4)	250	*Rep. Bob Traxler (D-8)	5,250
*Rep. Stephen Neal (D-5)		Rep. Guy Vander Jagt (R-9)	200
*Rep. Gene Johnston (R-6)	500	*Rep. Donald Albosta (D-10)	2,800
*Rep. Charles Rose (D-7)		*Rep. Robert Davis (R-11)	500
Rep. James Martin (R-9)	1,000	Rep. John Dingell (D-16)	1,650
Rep. James Broyhill (R-10)	500		
*Rep. Wm. Hendon (R-11)	1,000	**Minnesota**	
		*Sen. David Durenberger (R)	
Kentucky		Sen. Rudy Boschwitz (R)	196
*Sen. Walter Huddleston (D)		Rep. Arlen Erdahl (R-1)	500
*Rep. Carroll Hubbard (D-1)	450	Rep. Tom Hagedorn (R-2)	500
*Rep. William Natcher (D-2)		Rep. Bill Frenzel (R-3)	500
*Rep. Gene Snyder (R-4)	1,200	*Rep. Vin Weber (R-6)	12,450
*Rep. Harold Rogers (R-5)	1,750	*Rep. Arlan Stangeland (R-7)	500
Rep. Larry Hopkins (R-6)	700	Rep. James Oberstar (D-8)	950
Louisiana		**Mississippi**	
*Sen. J. Bennett Johnston (D)		Rep. Jamie Whitten (D-1)	500
Rep. Robert Livingston (R-1)	375	Rep. David Bowen (D-2)	200
*Rep. W. J. Tauzin (D-3)	1,300	*Rep. G. V. Montgomery D-3)	
*Rep. Jerry Huckaby (D-5)	500	*Rep. Trent Lott (R-5)	200
Rep. W. Henson Moore (R-6)	400		
*Rep. John Breaux (D-7)	1,300	**Missouri**	
Rep. Gillis Long (D-8)	750	*Sen. John C. Danforth	
		*Senator Thomas Eagleton (D)	26,444
Maine		Rep. Robert Young (D-2)	350
*Sen. William Cohen (R)		*Rep. Ike Skelton (D-4)	
*Rep. David Emery (R-1)		Rep. Thomas Coleman (R-6)	300
*Rep. Olympia Snowe (R-2)	750	*Rep. Gene Taylor (R-7)	400
		*Rep. Wendell Bailey (R-8)	1,000
Maryland		*Rep. Harold Volkmer (D-9)	32,186
*Rep. Roy Dyson (D-1)		*Rep. William Emerson (R-10)	
*Rep. Marjorie Holt (R-4)	200		
*Rep. Beverly Byron (D-6)			

RECIPIENT OF SUPPORT	TOTAL	RECIPIENT OF SUPPORT	TOTAL
North Dakota		**Pennsylvania**	
Sen. Mark Andrews (R)	2,750	Sen. Arlen Spector (R)	5,000
*Sen. Quentin Burdick (D)		Rep. Ray Lederer (D-3)	250
		Rep. Charles Dougherty (R-4)	7,550
Ohio		Rep. Richard Schulze (R-5)	150
Rep. Thomas Luken (D-2)	500	*Rep. Gus Yatron (D-6)	
Rep. Tennyson Guyer (R-4)	250	Rep. James Coyne (R-8)	1,100
Rep. Delbert Latta (R-5)	400	*Rep. Bud Shuster (R-9)	500
*Rep. Bob McEwen (R-6)	750	*Rep. James Nelligan (R-11)	500
Rep. Clarence Brown (R-7)	1,000	*Rep. John Murtha (D-12)	800
Rep. Ed Weber (R-9)	6,950	Rep. Donald Ritter (R-15)	2,730
*Rep. Clarence Miller (R-10)	1,000	*Rep. Allen Ertel (D-17)	1,300
*Rep. John Ashbrook (R-17)	400	*Rep. Joseph Gaydos (D-20)	
*Rep. Douglas Applegate (D-18)	300	*Rep. Don Bailey (D-21)	1,800
Rep. Lyle Williams (R-19)	2,614	*Rep. Austin Murphy (D-22)	800
		*Rep. Wm. Clinger (R-23)	300
Oklahoma		Rep. Marc Marks (R-24)	1,150
*Sen. David Boren (D)		*Rep. Eugene Atkinson (D-25)	
*Sen. Donald Nickles (R)	1,806		
*Rep. James Jones (D-1)	500	**South Carolina**	
*Rep. Michael Synar (D-2)		*Sen. Strom Thurmond (R)	
*Rep. Wes Watkins (D-3)		*Sen. Ernest Hollings (D)	
*Rep. David McCurdy (D-4)	500	*Rep. Thomas Hartnett (R-1)	6,464
*Rep. Mickey Edwards (R-5)	1,200	*Rep. Floyd Spence (R-2)	2,614
*Rep. Glenn English (D-6)	500	*Rep. Butler Derrick (D-3)	250
		Rep. Carroll Campbell (R-4)	1,125
Oregon		*Rep. John Napier (R-6)	1,500
*Sen. Mark Hatfield (R)	61		
Sen. Bob Packwood (R)	2,200	**South Dakota**	
*Rep. Les AuCoin (D-1)	761	*Sen. James Abdnor (R)	30,589
*Rep. Dennis Smith (R-2)	13,500	*Rep. Thomas Daschle (D-1)	
Rep. Ronald Wyden (D-3)	500	*Rep. Clint Roberts (R-2)	4,453
Rep. James Weaver (D-4)	1,061		

RECIPIENT OF SUPPORT	TOTAL	RECIPIENT OF SUPPORT	TOTAL
Tennessee		**Virginia**	
*Sen. James Sasser	100	Sen. John Warner (R)	283
*Rep. James Quillen (R-1)	2,500	Rep. Paul Trible (R-1)	433
*Rep. John Duncan (R-2)	250	Rep. Wm. Whitehurst (R-2)	33
Rep. Marilyn Bouquard (D-3)	250	*Rep. Thomas Bliley (R-3)	2,750
*Rep. Wm. Boner (D-5)	800	*Rep. Robert Daniel (R-4)	2,383
*Rep. Robin Beard (R-6)	450	*Rep. Dan Daniel (D-5)	33
*Rep. Ed Jones (D-7)		Rep. Caldwell Butler (R-6)	33
		Rep. Kenneth Robinson (R-7)	33
Texas		Rep. Stan Parris (R-8)	9,478
*Sen. John Tower (R)		Rep. Wm. Wampler (R-9)	533
*Sen. Lloyd Bentsen (D)		Rep. Frank Wolf (R-10)	5,660
*Rep. Sam Hall, Jr. (D-1)			
*Rep. Charles Wilson (D-2)	500	**Washington**	
*Rep. James Collins (R-3)		*Sen. Henry Jackson (D)	
Rep. Ralph Hall (D-4)	1,250	Sen. Slade Gorton (R)	1,000
*Rep. Phil Gramm (D-6)	1,000	Rep. Allan Swift (D-2)	400
*Rep. Jack Fields (R-8)	23,327	*Rep. Don Bonker (D-3)	
Rep. Jack Brooks (D-9)	1,000	*Rep. Sidney Morrison (R-4)	500
*Rep. Marvin Leath (D-11)	750	*Rep. Thomas Foley (D-5)	1,400
Rep. Jim Wright (D-12)		Rep. Norman Dicks (D-6)	250
*Rep. Jack Hightower (D-13)			
*Rep. William Patman (D-14)		**West Virginia**	
*Rep. E. DeLe Garza (D-15)	3,000	*Sen. Jennings Randolph (D)	
Rep. Richard White (D-16)	500	*Sen. Robert Byrd (D)	
*Rep. Charles Stenholm (D-17)	800	*Rep. Robert Mollohan (D-1)	
*Rep. Kent Hance (D-19)	125	*Rep. Cleve Benedict (R-2)	5,709
*Rep. Tom Loeffler (R-21)	100	*Rep. Mick Staton (R-3)	
*Rep. Ron Paul (R-22)	1,000	*Rep. Nick Joe Rahall (D-4)	500
*Rep. Abraham Kazen, Jr. (D-23)			
Rep. Martin Forst (D-24)	100	**Wisconsin**	
		*Sen. William Proxmire (D)	
Utah		*Sen. Robert Kasten (R)	10,632
*Sen. Orrin Hatch (R)		*Rep. Thomas Petri (R-6)	
*Sen. Jake Gam (R)	3,000	*Rep. James Sensenbrenner (R-9)	1,000
*Rep. Dan Marriott (R-2)	1,500		
		Wyoming	
		*Sen. Malcolm Wallop (R)	
Vermont		Sen. Alan Simpson (R)	550
*Sen. Patrick Leahy (D)	1,500	*Rep. Richard Cheney (R)	100

BIBLIOGRAPHY

Beha, James A., III (1977). " 'And Nobody Can Get You Out': The Impact of a Mandatory Prison Sentence for the Illegal Carrying of a Firearm on the Use of Firearms and the Administration of Criminal Justice in Boston," Parts I and II, *Boston University Law Review.*

Bruce-Briggs, B. (1976). "The Great American Gun War," *The Public Interest.* No. 45, Fall, 1–26.

Cook, Philip J., special editor (1981). "Gun Control," *Annals* of the American Academy of Political and Social Science, May.

Cook, Philip J. (1981). "The Role of Firearms in Violent Crime: An Interpretive Review of the Literature, with Some New Findings and Suggestions for Future Research," Institute of Policy Sciences and Public Affairs, Duke University.

Cook, Philip J. and **Daniel Nagin** (1979). *Does the Weapon Matter?* Washington, D.C.: Institute for Law and Social Research.

Kennett, Lee and **James LaVerne Anderson** (1975). *The Gun in America: The Origins of a National Dilemma,* Greenwood Press, Westport, Conn.

Lizotte, Alan J. and **David J. Bordua** (1980). "Firearms Ownership for Sport and Protection: Two Divergent Models," *American Sociological Review.* Vol. 45, (April) pp. 224–229.

Newton, George D., Jr. and **Franklin E. Zimring** (1969). *Firearms and Violence in American Life.* Washington, D.C.: Government Printing Office.

Perrin, Noel (1979) *Giving Up the Gun: Japan's Reversion to the Sword, 1543-1879,* David R. Godine, Boston.

Wright, James D., P. H. Rossi, K. Daly, and **E. Weber-Burdin** (1981). *Weapons, Crime, and Violence in America: Literature Review and Research Agenda,* Social and Demographic Research Institute. Amherst: University of Massachusetts.

Zimring, Franklin (1972). "The Medium is the Message: Firearm Calibre as a Determinant of Death from Assault," *The Journal of Legal Studies.* 1(1), Jan., pp. 97–124.

Zimring, Franklin (1975). "Firearms and Federal Law: The Gun Control Act of 1968," *The Journal of Legal Studies.* IV(1), Jan., pp. 133–198.